Praise for *I*

"This series provides a practical and focused discussion of the leading issues in law today." – John V. Biernacki, Partner, Jones Day

"*Inside the Minds* draws from the collective experience of the best professionals. The books are informative from an academic, and, more importantly, practical perspective. I highly recommend them." – Keith M. Aurzada, Partner, Bryan Cave LLP

"Aspatore's *Inside the Minds* series provides practical, cutting edge advice from those with insight into the real world challenges that confront businesses in the global economy." – Michael Bednarek, Partner, Shearman & Sterling LLP

"What to read when you want to be in the know—topical, current, practical, and useful information on areas of the law that everyone is talking about." – Erika L. Morabito, Partner, Patton Boggs LLP

"Some of the best insight around from sources in the know" – Donald R. Kirk, Shareholder, Fowler White Boggs PA

"The *Inside the Minds* series provides a unique window into the strategic thinking of key players in business and law." – John M. Sylvester, Partner, K&L Gates LLP

"Comprehensive analysis and strategies you won't find anywhere else." – Stephen C. Stapleton, Of Counsel, Dykema Gossett PLLC

"The *Inside the Minds* series is a real hands-on, practical resource for cutting edge issues." – Trey Monsour, Partner, Haynes and Boone LLP

"A tremendous resource, amalgamating commentary from leading professionals that is presented in a concise, easy to read format." – Alan H. Aronson, Shareholder, Akerman Senterfitt

"Unique and invaluable opportunity to gain insight into the minds of experienced professionals." – Jura C. Zibas, Partner, Lewis Brisbois Bisgaard & Smith LLP

"A refreshing collection of strategic insights, not dreary commonplaces, from some of the best of the profession." – Roger J. Magnuson, Partner, Dorsey & Whitney LLP

"Provides valuable insights by experienced practitioners into practical and theoretical developments in today's ever-changing legal world." – Elizabeth Gray, Partner, Willkie, Farr & Gallagher LLP

"This series provides invaluable insight into the practical experiences of lawyers in the trenches." – Thomas H. Christopher, Partner, Kilpatrick Stockton LLP

ASPATORE

Aspatore Books, a Thomson Reuters business, exclusively publishes C-Level executives and partners from the world's most respected companies and law firms. Each publication provides professionals of all levels with proven business and legal intelligence from industry insiders—direct and unfiltered insight from those who know it best. Aspatore Books is committed to publishing an innovative line of business and legal titles that lay forth principles and offer insights that can have a direct financial impact on the reader's business objectives.

Each chapter in the *Inside the Minds* series offers thought leadership and expert analysis on an industry, profession, or topic, providing a future-oriented perspective and proven strategies for success. Each author has been selected based on their experience and C-Level standing within the business and legal communities. *Inside the Minds* was conceived to give a first-hand look into the leading minds of top business executives and lawyers worldwide, presenting an unprecedented collection of views on various industries and professions.

INSIDE THE MINDS

Health Care Law Enforcement and Compliance

Leading Lawyers on Understanding Recent Trends in Health Care Enforcement, Updating Compliance Programs, and Developing Client Strategies

2014 EDITION

ASPATORE

CONTENTS

Government Oversight of Long-Term Care Providers in the Post-ACA World

Terry Schneier

Partner

Lewis Brisbois Bisgaard & Smith LLP

ASPATORE

Introduction

In 2010, Congress passed The Patient Protection and Affordable Care Act of 2010[1] as amended by the Health Care and Education Reconciliation Act of 2010,[2] which is collectively known as the Affordable Care Act or ACA.[3] The passage of this Act significantly expanded compliance risks and requirements for long-term care providers in a number of ways.

Section 6101 of the ACA[4] is entitled: "Required Disclosure of Ownership and Additional Disclosable Parties Information for Skilled Nursing Facilities and Nursing Facilities." Prior to the passage of the ACA, these entities, as a requirement for participation in the Medicare and Medicaid programs, were required to disclose their ownership to the Centers for Medicare and Medicaid Services, the Department of Public Health, and the Department of Health Care Services as part of their licensing and certification requirements. Section 6101 of the ACA expanded both the amount of the required information to be disclosed and the recipients of that information.

Nursing facilities and skilled nursing facilities are required to make available the identity of and information concerning the following:

1. Each member of the governing body of the facility, including the name, title, and period of service of each member;
2. Each person or entity who is an officer, director, member, partner, trustee, or managing employee of the facility, including the name, title, and period of service of each such person or entity;
3. Each person or entity, including organizational structure, that exercises operational, financial or managerial control over the facility or any part of it, or provides policies or procedures for any of the operations of the facility, or provides financial or cash management services to the facility;
4. Each person or entity, including organizational structure, that leases or subleases real property to the facility, or owns a whole

---

[1] Patient Protection and Affordable Care Act, Pub. L. No. 111-148, 124 Stat. 119 (2010).

[2] Health Care and Education Reconciliation Act of 2010, Pub. L. 111-152, 124 Stat. 1029.

[3] Patient Protection and Affordable Care Act, Pub. L. No. 111-148, 124 Stat. 119 (2010).

[4] Patient Protection and Affordable Care Act, Pub. L. No. 111-148, § 6101, 124 Stat. 699 (2010).

or part interest equal to or exceeding 5 percent of the total value of such real property; and

5. Each person or entity, including organizational structure, that provides management or administrative services, management or clinical consulting services, or accounting or financial services to the facility.

These entities are required to disclose this information to HHS upon enrollment in the Medicare program and within thirty days of any change in the facility ownership or organizational structure.[5] Further, this information must be made available for inspection by the Secretary of HHS, the HHS Inspector General, the state, and the long-term care ombudsman. Finally, not only must these entities report this information to the public, but this provision also requires the posting, in a public place, of the availability to review upon request survey, certification, and complaint investigation reports from the three preceding years.

The ready availability of this information to the public has been a boon to plaintiff's elder abuse and neglect attorneys, who no longer have to request it in discovery in an elder abuse and neglect case. Pursuant to the Elder Abuse and Dependent Adult Civil Protection Act,[6] plaintiffs were required to plead and prove, to receive the enhanced remedies under the statute, either that an employee whose reckless, malicious, oppressive, or fraudulent conduct caused injury was an officer, director, or managing agent, or that an officer, director, or managing agent had advance knowledge of the unfitness of the employee and employed him or her with a knowing disregard for the rights and safety of others, authorized the wrongful conduct, or knew of the wrongful conduct and adopted or approved it. Where prior to its passage, plaintiff's attorneys were required to make showings of a basis for the recovery of enhanced remedies to discover ownership information, Section 6101[7] of the ACA now places in the public arena the identities of an expansive list of individuals who potentially become defendants in elder abuse and neglect litigation without the requirement that such a showing be made.

Section 6102 of the ACA[8] is entitled "Accountability Requirements for Skilled Nursing Facilities and Nursing Facilities" and represents the most

---

[5] 42 C.F.R.§§ 424, 455 (2013).
[6] CAL. WELF. & INST. CODE § 15657 (2013).
[7] § 6101, 124 Stat. 699.
[8] *Id.* at § 6102, 124 Stat. 702.

significant new requirement for these entities. Beginning on March 23, 2010 the entity that operates each Medicare and/or Medicaid certified facility is required to have, in operation, a compliance and ethics program that is effective in preventing and detecting criminal, civil, and administrative violations and in promoting quality of care.[9]

Federal Sentencing Guidelines

The creation of compliance programs is not new to health care, although it is new to long-term care facilities with the passage of the ACA. This trend toward compliance programs began with the Federal Sentencing Guidelines[10] for organizations convicted of criminal violations. These guidelines explicitly reward and provide reductions of fines and penalties for organizations that have effective compliance programs and which cooperate in investigations. In addition, the Office of Inspector General (OIG) has aggressively encouraged providers to implement these programs and has stated that providers lacking these programs risk more severe sanctions if enforcement actions become necessary.

The seven minimum objectives of the Federal Sentencing Guidelines form the current basis of the minimum requirements for a long-term care facility compliance plan:

1. The organization shall establish standards and procedures to prevent and detect criminal conduct.
2. The organization's governing authority shall be knowledgeable about the content and operation of the compliance and ethics program and shall exercise reasonable oversight with respect to the implementation and effectiveness of the compliance and ethics program.
3. The organization shall use reasonable efforts not to include within the substantial authority personnel of the organization any individual whom the organization knew, or should have known through the exercise of due diligence, has engaged in illegal activities or other conduct inconsistent with an effective compliance and ethics program.

---

[9] Although HHS was required, pursuant to the Act, to promulgate regulations pertaining to this program, such regulations have yet to be promulgated.
[10] U.S. SENTENCING GUIDELINES MANUAL § 8B2 (2009).

4. The organization shall take reasonable steps to communicate periodically and in a practical manner its standards and procedures, and other aspects of the compliance and ethics program, by conducting effective training programs and otherwise disseminating information appropriate to such individuals' respective roles and responsibilities.

5. The organization shall take reasonable steps to ensure that the organization's compliance and ethics program is followed, including monitoring and auditing to detect criminal conduct; to evaluate periodically the effectiveness of the organization's compliance and ethics program; and to have and publicize a system, which may include mechanisms that allow for anonymity or confidentiality, whereby the organization's employees and agents may report or seek guidance regarding potential or actual criminal conduct without fear of retaliation.

6. The organization's compliance and ethics program shall be promoted and enforced consistently throughout the organization through appropriate incentives to perform in accordance with the compliance and ethics program, and appropriate disciplinary measures for engaging in criminal conduct and for failing to take reasonable steps to prevent or detect criminal conduct.

7. After criminal conduct has been detected, the organization shall take reasonable steps to respond appropriately to the criminal conduct and to prevent further criminal conduct, including making any necessary modifications to the organization's compliance and ethics program.

OIG Compliance Guidance

The Federal Sentencing Guidelines are not specific to health care. To more specifically address compliance and ethics issues affecting health care entities, the Office of Inspector General published compliance guidance directed toward specific health care entities. In 2000 and again in 2008, the OIG published compliance guidance directed at nursing facilities, and identified a number of specific risk areas that fall into the following categories: quality of care; resident's rights; billing and cost reporting; employee screening; kickbacks, inducements, and self-referrals; record-keeping; and fraud and abuse.

Quality of Care

Quality of care in long-term care facilities has long been a focus of regulatory oversight by CMS through its state survey agencies. Federal law requires that "each resident must receive and the facility must provide the necessary care and services to attain or maintain the highest practicable physical, mental, and psychosocial well-being, in accordance with the comprehensive assessment and plan of care."[11] A finding of substandard quality of care subjects a long-term care facility to deficiencies that must be corrected to maintain certification as well as remedies for the period of noncompliance. The post-ACA focus on quality of care has ratcheted up the number and severity of deficiencies, the severity of the remedies imposed, and a focus on whether quality of care deficiencies in and of themselves may constitute fraud.

Resident's Rights

Both federal and state laws have long been in place to protect a resident's rights. Following the passage of the ACA, however, more stringent requirements against the use of restraints have been put in place. Additionally, state surveyors appear to be laser focused on the issue of abuse of residents in long-term care facilities, the investigation of allegations of abuse, and whether those investigations meet the strict time frames set out in the regulation.[12]

Additionally, Section 6703 of the ACA[13] requires the reporting of "any reasonable suspicion...against any individual who is a resident of, or is receiving care from, the facility." If there is physical injury, the report must be made to the Secretary of HHS and to one or more police agencies within two hours of forming the suspicion. In the absence of physical injury, the time frame for reporting is twenty-four hours. A nursing facility may be found deficient both for permitting an injury to occur and for failing to report an injury in the regulatory time frames. An individual who is required to report and who fails to do so is subject to a civil money penalty of not

---

[11] 42 C.F.R. § 425 (2013).

[12] Anecdotally, a larger percentage of deficiencies and citations appear to have been issued for resident rights violations subsequent to the passage of the ACA.

[13] Patient Protection and Affordable Care Act, Pub. L. No. 111-148, § 6703, 124 Stat. 782 (2010).

more than $200,000 and may be excluded from participation in Medicare and Medicaid. Penalties up to $300,000 may be assessed if the failure to report exacerbates the harm to the victim of the crime or results in harm to another individual. Finally, long-term care facilities may not retaliate against any employee who makes a lawful report.

Billing and Cost Reporting

Billing and coding issues are a significant focus of the OIG and must be a major component of any long-term care compliance plan. The OIG has identified a series of reporting risk issues, including billing for items and services not rendered, submitting claims for items and services that are not medically necessary, submitting claims to Medicare Part A for residents who are not eligible for Part A coverage, and duplicate billing. As discussed below, violations in these areas may subject a provider to civil and criminal penalties under a variety of federal statutes.

Employee Screening

Employee screening is critically important in the wake of the passage of the ACA. Long-term care facilities must ensure that their employees have current licenses and certifications and have not been convicted of an offense that would preclude their employment in a nursing facility or exclude them from participation in a governmental health care program. To that end, the federal government maintains a list of excluded individuals for both employees and independent contractors, and employees must be checked against that list both prior to hire and then on a regular basis thereafter.

Kickbacks, Inducements, and Self-Referrals

Nursing facilities should have policies in place to ensure compliance with the federal Anti-Kickback Statute,[14] the Stark Law,[15] and other federal and state fraud and abuse laws. Any and all facility contracts and arrangements with actual or potential referral sources must be compliant with these laws. If a nursing facility discovers credible evidence of misconduct that violates civil,

---

[14] 42 U.S.C. § 1320a-7b (2012).
[15] 42 U.S.C. § 1395nn (2012).

criminal, or administrative law, then the nursing facility must report the misconduct within sixty days to the appropriate state and federal authorities.

The OIG has identified practices that could subject a nursing facility to liability under the Federal Anti-Kickback Statute and cautions vigilance about them:

a. Free goods and services may constitute a benefit to a recipient and may amount to a prohibited remuneration under the Federal Anti-Kickback Statute[16] if the purpose of the conferred benefit is to generate referrals. Even seemingly minor gifts to potential referrals of food items or other small tokens should be examined for potential violation.

b. Service contracts with physicians or non-physicians must be arm's-length transactions and include compensation at fair market value.

c. Although discounts are an exception under the Federal Anti-Kickback Statute, these discounts must be in the form of a reduced price for a good or service made in an arm's-length transaction and must be properly disclosed on all appropriate cost reports and claims.

d. Soliciting or receiving benefits from a hospice that might influence a nursing facility's decision to do business with that hospice may subject both the nursing facility and the hospice to penalties under the Federal Anti-Kickback Statute.

e. Reserved bed payments from hospitals may implicate the Federal Anti-Kickback Statute if the benefits conferred are for the purpose of inducing referrals.

Nursing facilities are required to comply with the requirements of The Health Insurance Portability and Accountability Act of 1996 (HIPAA)[17] rules, although according to the HIPAA "Privacy Rule"[18] and the HIPAA "Security Rule,"[19] facilities have some flexibility to create policies and procedures to ensure the privacy and confidentiality of health information that are tailored to their facility.

---

[16] 42 U.S.C. § 1320a-7b (2012).

[17] 45 C.F.R. § 160 (2013).

[18] *Id.* at §§ 160, 164.102-164.106, 164.500-164.534.

[19] *Id.* at §§ 160, 164.102-164.106, 16.302-16.318..

Record Keeping

Section 6106 of the ACA ensures staffing accountability for skilled nursing and nursing facilities by requiring a daily electronic submission of direct care staffing information to HHS. Each facility must specify the category of work each certified employee performs, include resident census and case mix data, include a regular reporting schedule, and include information on employee turnover and tenure. This additional information supplements the prior requirement to submit staffing hours to HHS, as well as the 2000 requirement set forth in the California Health & Safety Code20 that the minimum number of nursing hours per patient required in skilled nursing facilities shall be 3.2 hours. Once again, a nursing facility may be found deficient both for failing to staff appropriately and for failing to report properly to HHS.

Fraud and Abuse

CMS, through its contracted state agencies (state Department of Public Health, for example), conducts annual surveys of skilled nursing and nursing facilities to determine compliance with the Medicare and Medicaid conditions of participation. If, as a result of these surveys, the surveyors note any deficiencies according to federal or state regulations, these deficiencies must be corrected through the mechanism of a Plan of Correction and potential re-survey to remain in compliance with the conditions of participation. A facility that remains out of compliance is subject to a civil money penalty, denial of payment for new admissions, and ultimately, termination from participation in the Medicare and Medicaid programs. Additionally, these state agencies conduct complaint investigations and issue deficiencies and citations based upon any regulatory violations that arise from those investigations, and facilities must respond as they do to survey deficiencies.

Government Enforcement

Over the past twenty years, Congress has steadily expanded enforcement agency enforcement tools, while at the same time it has limited the provider's defenses. Congress passed the Fraud Enforcement and Recovery Act of 2009[21] to enhance criminal penalties and enforcement of existing

---

[20] CAL. HEALTH & SAFETY CODE § 1276.5(a) (2013).
[21] Fraud Enforcement and Recovery Act of 2009, Pub. L. 111-21, 123 Stat. 1617.

federal fraud laws and, in the process, broadened the scope of the False Claims Act[22] and overruled several court decisions interpreting the False Claims Act in favor of defendants.

The United States Department of Justice has called 2014 the "banner year" for False Claims Act, Healthcare Fraud, Procurement Fraud and "Other" Fraud (such as wire and mail fraud) affecting health care providers. For health care fraud alone, the United States Department of Justice collected $2.6 billion during 2013 with this being the fourth straight year with collections exceeding $2 billion. The government also collected $3.8 billion from False Claims Act cases stemming from "whistleblower" actions in which a whistleblower receives a monetary award (a percentage of the recovery) for bringing the matter to the government's attention. Most of the time the whistleblower is a disgruntled employee of the health care entity.

Common fraud cases that have arisen since the passage of the ACA are those where health care providers took referral kickbacks from patients or billed Medicare for medical services that were not provided. Because not all of the requirements have been implemented and the statute of limitations for fraud is generally five years, we have yet to see the extent to which the government will prosecute fraud with a focus on large monetary recoveries.

Criminal fraud is based upon both knowledge and intent, while civil fraud requires only a degree of recklessness. With either criminal or civil fraud, deliberate ignorance is never a defense. When advising clients with regard to their billing practices, oversight and training, the following questions can inform that advice:

1. What are the billing practices of the health care entity, and what is the extent of the client's oversight and authorization of those practices?
2. What safeguards are in place to ensure that medical services are correctly described and reported—i.e., who is submitting, how is the submission reviewed, and who is authorized to submit?
3. Prompt reporting of any discrepancy is critical to avoiding criminal charges. What mechanisms are in place to ensure that any error is immediately reported? How are employees trained to disclose errors immediately without fear of reprisal?

---

[22] 31 U.S.C. §§ 3729-3733 (2013).

4. Training is critical, so what training programs are in place and how often does training occur? How does the client ensure that the trainees really understood? An interactive video with scoring may be the most effective training tool.

5. Has a compliance helpline or hotline been set up for the entity? How often has the helpline or hotline been used, and is information about how to access it posted where the people who need to use it can see it? Is there a non-retaliation policy for reporting suspected billing errors or fraud?

The federal government has also stepped up its enforcement of breaches of the privacy of protected health information. In 2000, HHS published the first comprehensive federal privacy regulations implementing HIPAA.[23] The rules were then substantially revised in 2010 as a result of the requirements set forth in the HITECH Act.[24] HIPAA included federal rules regarding the electronic submission of electronic health information. HITECH imposed these rules directly upon business associates (including claims processors, accountants, attorneys, or consultants who work for or with the long-term care providers.) For the first time, attorneys representing long-term care providers were required to maintain the privacy of protected health information used in litigation, pursuant to statute.

HIPAA created several new criminal offenses, including a new health care fraud offense with enhanced criminal penalties. HIPAA also authorized federal prosecutors to obtain injunctions and freeze the assets of persons or entities alleged to commit health care offenses and to issue administrative subpoenas in an investigation without a grand jury, and directed judges sentencing convicted federal health care offenders to impose criminal forfeiture on assets obtained as a result of the fraud. HIPAA further expanded the OIG's broad authority to impose civil money penalties and exclude providers from participating in Medicare.

Just in the last year, HHS has imposed significant civil money penalties against health care entities who failed to protect personal health care

---

[23] Health Insurance Portability and Accountability Act of 1996, Pub. L. 104-191, §§ 261-64, 110 Stat. 1936.

[24] Health Information Technology for Economic and Clinical Health Act of 2009, Pub. L. 111-5, 123 Stat. 226.

information (PHI) and has stated its intention to continue to do so. For example, HHS imposed a fine of $4,300,000 against CIGNET as a result of an online database application error, of $1,700,000 against the Alaska Department of Health and Human Services as a result of the theft of an unencrypted USB hard drive along with poor policies and risk analysis, against WellPoint of $1,700,000 because it did not have technical safeguards in place to verify either the person or entity seeking access to PHI in its database, Blue Cross Blue Shield of Tennessee as a result of the theft of fifty-seven unencrypted hard drives, and Affinity Health Plan was fined $1,215,780 when it returned photocopiers without erasing the hard drives. Smaller fines were levied against various hospitals for breaches of unsecured PHI along with inadequate safeguarding of the data and inadequate risk analysis by the entities.

In addition to the False Claim Act and HIPAA, the federal government relies on additional statutes to prosecute health care providers for violations of federal law. The federal statutes used by the government to fight alleged health care fraud include:

1. The Civil False Claim Act[25] and the Criminal False Claims Act[26]
2. Criminal False Claims Relating to Medicare/Medicaid[27]
3. The Anti-Kickback Statute[28]
4. Physician Self-Referral (Stark) Prohibitions[29]
5. CMP Law[30]
6. Payment Suspension[31]
7. Racketeer Influenced and Corrupt Organizations Act[32]
8. Mail and Wire Fraud[33]

Providers of health care are always vulnerable to federal enforcement actions, deserved or not. The OIG has made it its primary focus in 2014 to identify and punish fraud and abuse. Long-term care providers must put

---

[25] 31 USC § 3729.
[26] 18 USC § 287.
[27] 42 USC § 1320a-7b(a).
[28] 42 USC § 1320a-7b(b).
[29] 42 USC § 1320a-7.
[30] 42 USC § 1320a-7a.
[31] 42 CFR § 405.370.
[32] 18 USC § 1964.
[33] 18 USC §§ 1341, 1343.

processes in place to identify and investigate any potential fraud or abuse, and to seek the advice of counsel when that identification is made so as to immediately address the issues and minimize the penalties to the entity and to the individuals who operate it.

Conclusion

In the post-ACA world, the focus of long-term care providers must be transparency and compliance. In the short term, all long-term care providers must put compliance programs in place that provide for a compliance structure, training, and reporting. Once HHS promulgates the compliance program regulations that have long been promised and which are overdue, there will undoubtedly be additional requirements for compliance and additional and increased sanctions for failure to comply with these requirements.

Health care providers and their attorneys must understand and appreciate the nature and extent of the civil and criminal penalties for noncompliance. When a government entity seeks an interview or subpoenas documents, these provider/clients must be educated to seek the advice of counsel prior to responding, as a misstep can result in substantial penalties. Attorneys working in this area of the law must be aware of the constantly changing landscape of compliance and regulation and work with their long-term care clients to appreciate and respond to that changing landscape.

Key Takeaways

- If you represent a nursing facility, advise them that the ACA requires these facilities to now disclose their ownership information to numerous more agencies than before and with more detail.
- Long-term care facilities are required by the ACA to have compliance programs. Until HHS promulgates regulations, become familiar with the 2009 Federal Sentencing Guidelines, as they are now the basis for nursing facilities' compliance programs.
- Staff of nursing facilities can be found in violation of federal regulations for not only allowing abuse to occur to a patient but also failing to report it in a timely manner. Failure to report abuse can lead to a fine of up to $300,000, depending on the circumstances.

- Keep in mind: courts have not decided in favor of defendants recently in terms of fraud cases. The passage of the Fraud Enforcement and Recovery Act of 2009 broadened the reach of the False Claims Act, making it more difficult for defendants to win their cases.

- Long-term care clients should be counseled to consult counsel any time they are contacted by the state or federal Departments of Justice, HHS or the Office of Inspector General with a request for documents or an interview, due to the danger of civil or criminal penalties for violations of federal statutes.

Terry Schneier, partner in the firm of Lewis Brisbois Bisgaard & Smith LLP, also serves as the firm's co-chair of the Healthcare Regulatory and Compliance Practice Group. She has extensive experience in the areas of health care regulatory litigation and compliance. Ms. Schneier successfully tried a Class A citation case, had the citation deleted, and has litigated state and federal deficiency citations issued to skilled nursing and assisted-living communities against the California Department of Public Health, the California Attorney General's Bureau of Medicare Fraud and Abuse, the Arizona Department of Health Services, the US Department of Health and Human Services, and the Centers for Medicare and Medicaid Services. Ms. Schneier has handled licensing issues against state nursing and medical boards on behalf of nurses and physicians, as well as litigating Medicaid payment matters with the Department of Health Services. Ms. Schneier has negotiated numerous class and penalty reductions with deputy attorneys general and DPH staff attorneys.

In addition to litigation, Ms. Schneier performs facility investigations of allegations of abuse, unusual occurrence or immediate jeopardy, and drafts informal dispute resolution and citation review arguments based upon complaint and survey deficiencies. She has represented communities and their employees in criminal investigations. Ms. Schneier has assisted with drafting policies and procedures and reviewing existing ones to determine their necessity in accordance with state and federal regulations. She has in-serviced community staff on a variety of reporting and documentation issues. Ms. Schneier completed a 1,000-hour Administrator in Training Program at Orange Tree Nursing Center and is now eligible to take the state and federal examinations for nursing home licensure. She is admitted to practice law in California, Arizona, and Nevada.

Acknowledgment: *I would like to acknowledge the contributions of Kathleen Bliss—a partner at Lewis Brisbois Bisgaard & Smith LLP, who serves as Co-Chair of the*

Healthcare Regulatory and Compliance Practice Group; Chair of the White Collar and Financial Crimes Practice Group; vice-Chair of the Indian Nations Law and Policy Practice Group. Ms. Bliss is also a former federal prosecutor and Assistant US Attorney for the District of Nevada assigned to the Organized Crime Strike Force—for contributions to sections on government enforcement and client advice.

I would also like to acknowledge the contributions of Matthew Izu, an associate at Lewis Brisbois Bisgaard & Smith LLP, for his assistance with research and cite checking.

The Open Payments Program: Enforcing Transparency Under the Sunshine Law

Ruth E. Granfors

Partner

Kirkpatrick & Lockhart LLP

ASPATORE

Introduction

One of the new "buzzwords" in health care reform is "transparency." Transparency generally means required disclosure of certain information formerly considered confidential or of little interest to the public. Revealing this information, or making it available in a public format, may become one of the most heavily used tools for improving health care quality, lowering health care costs, and engaging consumers in decision making about their health care choices. Transparency is used in multiple sections of the Patient Protection and Affordable Care Act (ACA),[1] but one new area has received attention. Under what is often referred to as the "Physician Payments Sunshine Act" section of the ACA,[2] the Centers for Medicare and Medicaid Services (CMS) have established the "Open Payments" program.

The law mandates applicable manufacturers and applicable group purchasing organizations (collectively, reporting entities) to disclose payments of cash or other "transfers of value" to physicians and teaching hospitals and to report physician investment and ownership in reporting entities.[3] Under this provision, CMS published final regulations on February 8, 2013 and established the Open Payments program.[4] The Open Payments program is a health care integrity tool, but CMS explains that required reporting does not imply that an inappropriate payment has been made.

The Open Payments requirements of the ACA stem from an Institute of Medicine report entitled "Conflict of Interest in Medical Research, Education, and Practice" (IOM Report).[5] The IOM Report, published in April 2009, recommends that Congress create a national public reporting program whereby pharmaceutical, medical device, and biotechnology programs would disclose payments to "physicians and other prescribers,

---

[1] Patient Protection and Affordable Care Act, Pub. L. No. 111-148. 124 Stat. 119 (2010).

[2] Section 6002 of the ACA, entitled "Transparency Reports and Reporting of Physician Ownership or Investment Interests", amended section 1128 of the Social Security Act to add section 1128G. Patient Protection and Affordable Care Act § 6002; 42 U.S.C. § 1320a-7h.

[3] 42 U.S.C. § 1320a-7h.

[4] See 42 C.F.R. §§ 402.1, 402.105, 403.900-914.

[5] The IOM Report is available for download on the IOM website. INSTITUTE OF MEDICINE, CONFLICT OF INTEREST IN MEDICAL RESEARCH, EDUCATION, AND PRACTICE (2009), available at http://www.iom.edu/Reports/2009/Conflict-of-Interest-in-Medical-Research-Education-and-Practice.aspx (last visited June 9, 2014).

biomedical researchers, health care institutions, professional societies, patient advocacy and disease-specific groups, providers of continuing medical education, and foundations created by any of these entities."[6] This is one of a number of recommendations, which include development of conflicts of interest policies by hospitals and research institutions; development of standard content, format, and procedure for disclosing financial relationships; and development of educational programs for physicians on conflicts of interest.

This is not the first foray of the government into regulation of financial relationships in health care. The Physician Self-Referral Law (Stark Law)[7] and Anti-Kickback Statute[8] are two of the most pervasive health care law enforcement areas. Both of these laws address certain financial relationships between physicians and other entities and referrals from physicians to those entities. The Stark Law specifically prohibits physician referrals for services that are reimbursed by Medicare or Medicaid unless the physician-entity relationship meets an exception.[9] In addition, the Office of Inspector General (OIG) for the Department of Health and Human Services (HHS) addresses joint ventures with physicians and disclosure to patients of related financial interests in the supplemental compliance program guidance for hospitals.[10] The OIG also mentions kickbacks and other illegal remuneration as a risk area in the compliance program guidance for pharmaceutical companies and improper inducements, kickbacks, and self-referrals in the compliance program guidance for individual and small group physician practices.[11] In other words, the federal government, through CMS and the OIG, has viewed financial relationships between physicians and other entities with some skepticism and concern for the public fisc. Now, with the Open Payments program, the federal government is requiring that certain relationships be made public so that consumers can decide for themselves whether a physician or teaching hospital is unduly influenced by parties that pay them for legitimate services, such as research or consulting.

---

[6] IOM Report, p.94, Recommendation 3.4.

[7] 42 U.S.C. § 1395nn.

[8] *Id.* § 1320a-7b(b).

[9] *Id.* § 1395nn(a).

[10] The supplemental compliance guidance is available on the OIC website. OIG Supplemental Compliance Program Guidance for Hospitals, 70 Fed. Reg. 4858 (Jan. 31, 2005), *available at* http://oig.hhs.gov/compliance/compliance-guidance/index.asp.

[11] *Id.*

On the private side, the pharmaceutical and device manufacturers have encouraged self-regulation of company relationships with health care providers. The Pharmaceutical and Research Manufacturers of America (PhRMA) has had a code of ethics in place since 2002. In January 2009, it revised and updated the "Code on Interactions with Healthcare Professionals."[12] The PhRMA Code[13] addresses numerous issues regarding financial relationships between physicians and pharmaceutical companies, including disclosure by physicians who serve on committees that work on formularies or clinical practice guidelines to the committees on which they serve. Similarly, the Advanced Medical Technology Association (AdvaMed) has a Code of Ethics on Interactions with Health Care Professionals.[14] AdvaMed emphasizes that relationships between medical technology companies and health care professionals are necessary and should promote the best interest of the patients, but it acknowledges: "To ensure that these collaborative relationships meet high ethical standards, they must be conducted with appropriate transparency and in compliance with applicable laws, regulations and government guidance."[15] However, none of the central principles in either the PhRMA Code or the AdvaMed Code directly address disclosure of financial relationships to the public. In part, as recommended by the IOM Report, a centralized national system and standard format for reporting is needed to provide regular access to this information by the public.

The purpose of the Open Payments program is to provide the consumer with knowledge of potential conflicts of interest of prescribing physicians and teaching hospitals that could affect treatment and clinical research decisions.[16] It is a likely consequence that the Open Payments program may curb certain financial transfers between reporting entities and covered recipients. Certainly, the law could affect transfers of value that would raise compliance concerns with respect to the Stark Law[17] or Anti-Kickback Statute.[18] A requirement to report when the transfer of value is questionable—for

---

[12] Code *on Interactions with Health Care Professionals*, PHRMA, http://www.phrma.org/principles-guidelines/code-on-interactions-with-health-care-professionals (last visited June 9, 2014).

[13] *Id.*

[14] *Code of Ethics*, ADVAMED, http://advamed.org/issues/1/code-of-ethics (last visited June 9, 2014).

[15] *Id.*

[16] *See* 78 Fed. Reg. 9458 (Feb. 8, 2013).

[17] 42 U.S.C. § 1395nn (2012).

[18] 42 U.S.C. § 1320a-7b (2012).

example, a consulting fee from a pharmaceutical company does not satisfy fair market value—may cause a manufacturer not to enter into such an arrangement. The questions these relationships would raise may not be worth it to the reporting entities and any attempt to avoid reporting would be viewed as a knowing failure under the law. As explained at the end of this chapter, penalties for knowing failure to disclose are significant.

Open Payments Requirements

Who Is Affected?

The Open Payments program affects two categories of persons: (1) those who are obligated to report, or the reporting entities, and (2) those about whom reports are made, i.e., the covered recipients. Stated another way, the program involves those entities required to disclose the transfer of a payment or other items of value and those individuals or entities who become the subject of the Open Payments report.

The reporting entities are: (1) "applicable manufacturers," and (2) "applicable group purchasing organizations." The subjects of the reports or covered recipients are: (1) physicians, and sometimes their immediate family members, and (2) teaching hospitals.

Applicable Manufacturers

An applicable manufacturer meets these characteristics:

a. The entity is engaged in the following activities: the production, preparation, propagation, compounding, or conversion of a covered drug, device, biological, or medical supply (collectively, covered products), to be used by persons other than the entity's own patients. CMS calls these entities Type 1 manufacturers.

Based on this definition, CMS clarified in the final regulations that Type 1 manufacturers may include repackagers, relabelers, and kit assemblers, if the entity engaging in repackaging, relabeling or assembling holds title to the covered product. Thus, certain distributors and wholesalers may be "manufacturers" for purposes of Open Payments, depending on whether they hold title to the products distributed. Possession of a covered product does not necessarily define title. The question of who holds title should be addressed in any contract between the manufacturer and wholesaler or distributor.

Alternatively, if an entity is under common ownership with a Type 1 manufacturer and the entity provides assistance or support to the Type 1 manufacturer on the listed activities (i.e., production, preparation, propagation, etc.), this other entity may be covered by the law. CMS calls these entities Type 2 manufacturers.

b.   The entity must operate in the United States. The regulation states that this means the entity either has a physical location within the United States (including a territory, possession, or commonwealth of the United States), *or* it conducts covered activities within the United States, directly or through a legally authorized agent.[19]

Applicable GPOs

An applicable GPO meets these characteristics:

a.   The entity engages in the purchasing, arranging for, or negotiating the purchase of a covered product for a group of individuals or entities, other than for the entity's sole use.
b.   The entity must operate in the United States. This means that it either is physically located in the United States (including a territory, possession, or commonwealth of the United States), or "otherwise conducts activities within the United States or in a territory, possession or commonwealth of the United States, either directly or through a legally-authorized agent."[20]

The other affected group to be discussed is covered recipients. These recipients are the subject of the reports made by applicable manufacturers and applicable GPOs. Covered recipients have a right to correct information that is reported about them. As stated above, covered recipients are physicians, immediate family members of a physician owner or investor, and teaching hospitals.

---

[19] *See* 42 C.F.R. § 403.902.
[20] *Id.*

Physicians and Immediate Family Members

A "physician" is defined by reference to the Social Security Act definition for Medicare purposes, which includes an individual licensed as a/an:

1. Medical doctor (MD),
2. Doctor of osteopathy (DO),
3. Dentist or dental surgeon,
4. Podiatrist,
5. Optometrist, or
6. Chiropractor.[21]

Under the regulations, a physician does not include a resident. CMS recognizes that some states do not permit residents to obtain a license so it excludes all residents from the definition to avoid different requirements from state to state. In addition, a physician is not a covered recipient for purposes of reports made by an employer, as defined by the common law employer-employee relationship and recognized as an employee by the IRS.

For example, a manufacturer need not report on compensation or other transfers of value made to an employed physician. However, it would need to report such transfers to a contracted physician performing consulting services for the manufacturer.

A physician's immediate family members include the physician's

1. Spouse,
2. Natural or adoptive parent,
3. Natural or adoptive child,
4. Natural or adoptive sibling,
5. Stepparent,
6. Stepchild,
7. Stepbrother or stepsister,
8. An in-law,
9. A grandparent or the spouse of a grandparent, and
10. A grandchild or spouse of a grandchild.

---

[21] *See* 42 U.S.C. § 1395x(r).

Teaching Hospitals

A teaching hospital is a hospital that received a Medicare payment for: (1) direct graduate medical education (GME), or (2) indirect medical education (IME) under either (a) the inpatient prospective payment system (IPPS) for acute care hospitals or (b) the prospective payment system for psychiatric hospitals during the prior calendar year. CMS plans to publish a list of such hospitals for each reporting year on its website.[22]

Covered Drugs, Devices, Biologicals or Medical Supplies (Covered Products)

Applicable manufacturers and applicable GPOs are only subject to Open Payments requirements if they engage in the covered activities with respect to certain drugs, devices, biologicals, and medical supplies (collectively, "covered products"). Covered products must meet the following requirements:

1. The product is one for which Medicare, Medicaid, or the Children's Health Insurance Program (CHIP) reimbursement is available,
2. If the product is a drug or biological it must be one that, by law, requires a prescription to be dispensed, and
3. If the product is a device or medical supply, it must be one that requires either premarket approval by, or premarket notification to, the Food and Drug Administration (FDA).

Availability of Medicare, Medicaid, or CHIP Payment

The product is a covered drug, device, biological, or medical supply when reimbursement through Medicare, Medicaid, or CHIP is available, regardless of whether a particular manufacturer's product is actually reimbursed through one of those payors. In response to comments that available payment should be limited to items that are reimbursed directly and not indirectly as part of a bundled payment, Medicare stated:

> [W]e do not agree with the suggestions to interpret payment availability as being limited to those provided

---

[22] Teaching Hospitals, CMS.GOV, http://www.cms.gov/Regulations-and-Guidance/Legislation/National-Physician-Payment-Transparency-Program/Teaching-Hospitals.html (last visited June 9, 2014).

separately, rather than through a bundled payment. We recognize that it is not always clear whether a product is paid through a bundle, making it difficult to establish whether payment is available. We also recognize that this expands the number of products meeting the definition of covered drug, device, biological or medical supply. However, bundled payments constitute a significant portion of Medicare reimbursement and excluding products that are reimbursed only as part of bundled payments would exclude manufacturers of products who have historically had significant relationships with physicians and teaching hospitals.[23]

An example provided in the regulations is an implantable device that may be covered by payment under the IPPS. Similarly, CMS clarified that a device that is used as part of a covered service—for example, an X-ray machine—is a covered product because Medicare payment is available for the radiology service.

In contrast, CMS stated:

> Raw materials and components often do not meet the definition of covered drug, device, biological, or medical supply because payment is not available for them in their component form under Medicare, Medicaid or CHIP. Entities that only manufacture raw materials or components, which are not themselves covered products, will not be required to report unless they are [a Type 2 manufacturer].[24]

Limitation on Drugs and Biologicals

A drug or biological is a covered product only if the requisite reimbursement is available through Medicare, Medicaid, or CHIP *and* a prescription is required for dispensing. Over-the-counter (OTC) drugs are not covered products. A pharmaceutical manufacturer that is in the business of OTC products only is not an applicable manufacturer covered by the law. But if the

---

[23] 78 Fed. Reg. 9465, 9466 (Feb. 8, 2013).
[24] 78 Fed. Reg. 9461 (Feb. 8, 2013).

manufacturer produces only one non-OTC drug, it becomes an applicable manufacturer required to report. However, CMS explains that a division of a manufacturer that does not engage in covered activities related to covered products need not report transfers of value. The question is how the entity is structured and whether the division of the entity engages in covered activities:

> In general, we believe that all payments or other transfers of value related to covered products should be reported, but that we should minimize the reporting of payments or other transfers of value unrelated to covered products. The final rule does not require entities under common ownership to report when they are not necessary or integral to manufacturing, and are not applicable manufacturers in and of themselves. However, an indirect payment or other transfer of value made to a covered recipient through an entity under common ownership that is not necessary or integral to the manufacturing process must still be reported as required for indirect payments or other transfers of value.[25]

Limitation on Devices and Medical Supplies

A device or medical supply is a covered product only if the requisite reimbursement is available through Medicare, Medicaid, or CHIP *and* the device or medical supply requires premarket approval by or premarket notification to the FDA. If a device requires premarket approval, it does not mean that the product is covered only after such FDA approval is received. The question is whether the device requires premarket approval and Medicare, Medicaid, or CHIP funding is available to pay for the device. Usually such funding is not available prior to approval, but CMS clarifies that some investigational studies provide for Medicare funding of the device under investigation. Where such funding is available prior to premarket approval, the device is a covered product and the manufacturer is required to report.

Information To Be Reported

The general rule is that applicable manufacturers and applicable GPOs report all "payments and transfers of value" they make to covered recipients. What

---

[25] 78 Fed. Reg. 9464 (Feb. 8, 2013).

are transfers of value? The federal government has defined the term broadly, but has more specifically defined what it is not. So, while the definition of "payment or other transfer of value" is simply defined as "a transfer of anything of value," and that could occur directly or indirectly, there are exclusions from required reporting.[26] For example, there is an exception for any transfer valued under $10, as long as aggregate transfers to the same covered recipient do not exceed an amount that is published annually.

In addition, a covered reporter is required to disclose any ownership or investment interest that a physician or immediate family member of the physician held in the covered reporter during the prior year. An ownership or investment interest does not include:

1. An interest held in a publicly traded security or mutual fund,
2. An interest that arises through an employee retirement plan because of the physician's or immediate family member's employment with the covered reporter,
3. Stock option or convertible securities prior to exercise of the option or conversion of the security to equity,
4. An unsecured loan that is subordinated to a credit facility, or
5. Any interest held by a physician or family member of which the reporting entity had no knowledge of the interest.

The reports about ownership/investment interests require disclosure of any direct or indirect payment or transfer of value made to the owner/investor by the covered reporter.

The Reporting Process

CMS has developed an online portal for reporting information in 2014 for calendar year 2013.[27] Applicable manufacturers and applicable GPOs are required to report the requested information each year for the prior year.

There is an exception to publication of information reported for research and development activities. Publication of information about a payment or

---

[26] 42 C.F.R. § 403.904(i).
[27] *Enterprise Portal*, CMS.GOV, https://portal.cms.gov/wps/portal/unauthportal/home/ (last visited June 9, 2014).

transfer of value by an applicable manufacturer to a covered recipient under a research or development agreement may be delayed if the transfer is related to (1) research or development on a new drug, device, biological or medical supply or (2) clinical investigation of a new drug, device, biological or medical supply. The delayed publication may occur no later than the earlier of the first publication date following either FDA approval, licensure or clearance of the new drug, device, biological or medical supply, or four calendar years after the date the payment or transfer of value was made.

Physicians and teaching hospitals are encouraged to register for access to the site so that information reported about them may be monitored for accuracy. Before the information is reported to the public, the recipient or subject of the report has an opportunity to dispute the information. Depending on how the dispute is resolved, the information may be corrected, removed from the portal, reported as is, or reported with an indication that it is under dispute.

Covered recipients should have an interest in knowing what is reported about them as it may influence perceptions about the physician or teaching hospital. In time, the information may be used in a variety of ways by patients, prospective patients, insurers, and government payors.

There is an exception to reporting by the following calendar year for research and development activities. Payments or transfers of value by an applicable manufacturer to a covered recipient under a research or development agreement may be delayed.

Preemption of State Laws

Some states have disclosure laws regarding physician relationships. For example, Pennsylvania requires any "practitioner of the healing arts" to disclose a financial interest or ownership in a facility or entity that provides health-related services or tests, pharmaceuticals, appliances or devices, or supply company to which the practitioner refers prior to the referral. So, for example, a physician who is employed by a hospital must disclose the relationship when the physician refers to the hospital. The practitioner is also required to advise the patient of the patient's freedom to choose another hospital.

The Open Payments program provides for preemption of certain state laws, but only if it is an obligation placed on an applicable manufacturer to report a payment or transfer of value to a covered recipient, regardless of how the report is to be made. So the Pennsylvania state law would not be preempted. Any reporting to a government agency based on public health and disease control activities or oversight (e.g., licensure or registration) also remains enforceable and is not preempted.

Penalties

The Open Payments program distinguishes between knowing and unknowing failure to comply with the requirements for reporting. An unknowing failure to report in accordance with the law may result in a civil money penalty of $1,000 to $10,000 per failure, not to exceed $150,000 in the aggregate. Whereas, a knowing failure to report in accordance with the law may result in a civil money penalty of $10,000 to $100,000 per failure, not to exceed $1,000,000 in the aggregate. It is important to note that these failures do not relate only to failure to file a report but also failure to report timely, accurately, or completely.

Under the regulations "know, knowing, or knowingly" means that a person:

    i.   Has actual knowledge of the information;

    ii.   Acts in deliberate ignorance of the truth or falsity of the information; or

    iii.   Acts in reckless disregard of the truth or falsity of the information.[28]

In addition, CMS has determined that "knowing" requires "no proof of a specific intent to defraud."[29]

Generally with a new program, CMS provides a period of learning to get reports accurate and complete. That would be expected in this situation as well. But covered reporters should take the time to comply with the law, ask questions if there are ambiguities or unusual situations, and adhere to the time frames established by CMS. Covered entities also need to understand

---

[28] 42 C.F.R. § 403.902.
[29] *Id.*

completely what is happening in the field with respect to sales people, business developers, and research units. Failure to report each payment or transfer of value could result in substantial penalties even if the entity is deemed not to have known of the failure.

Reporting entities should make the requirements under the Open Payments program part of their regular compliance programs, including any necessary training of individuals who have regular interactions with physicians and teaching hospitals. If payments are not properly reported, the failure may be detected in an audit, which is also authorized under the regulations. Depending on the circumstances, it could lead to an investigation under the Anti-Kickback Statute, which may carry additional penalties, and potential exclusion from government programs, in addition to the Open Payments fines for a knowing violation of the law.

Conclusion

Operation of the Open Payments program has begun and now is the time for reporting entities (manufacturers and GPOs) to develop reporting policies and procedures as part of a regular compliance program. This includes understanding whether your organization is an *applicable* manufacturer or *applicable* GPO subject to the requirements, whether transfers of value are being made to physicians or teaching hospitals, and whether physicians have an investment interest in your organization. Applicable manufacturers and applicable GPOs should also consider whether transfers of value are clearly permissible under other state and federal laws that regulate such payments, such as the Stark Law[30] and Anti-Kickback Statute.[31]

Physicians and teaching hospitals should assign an individual in the organization or physician's office to determine whether they are receiving transfers of value from applicable manufacturers or applicable GPOs. Physicians and teaching hospitals should monitor the reports that manufacturers and GPOs make to the federal government to ensure that information that is reported is consistent with their records of receipt of any transfer of value.

---

[30] 42 U.S.C. § 1395nn (2012).
[31] *Id.* § 1320a-7b (2012).

At this point, enforcement of the law will likely be more lenient as reporting entities become familiar with the requirements and work through any difficulties in understanding the law and its applicability to the entity's operations. This law is part of the federal government's health care integrity program, however, so it is likely that enforcement will ramp up and several years from now, the federal government will look to penalize entities that are not compliant and look specifically for those manufacturers or GPOs that appear to be intentionally evading the law's obligations.

Key Takeaways

- Make sure your clients understand the purpose of the Open Payments Program. Its aim is to make public potential conflicts of interest between reporting entities (applicable manufacturers and applicable GPOs) and physicians, their immediate family members or teaching hospitals. Armed with the mandated reports, consumers will be able to make decisions about their treatment or participation in research.

- Two different kinds of people are affected by the Open Payments Program: the ones who must make a report and those that are the subject of the report—i.e., received a transfer of value from the reporter. The "reporting entities" include applicable manufacturers and applicable group purchasing organizations. The "covered recipients" include doctors, their immediate family members and teaching hospitals.

- It is important to note what constitutes a "covered product" as applicable manufacturers are subject to the law only if they are engaged in covered activities involving covered products. For example, OTC drugs are not covered products. The product must be available through Medicare or Medicaid and be prescribed by a doctor.

- CMS encourages doctors and hospitals to register with their online portal in an effort to ensure the information reported is accurate.

- Failure to comply with the Open Payments Program reporting requirements is accompanied by very serious consequences. An unknowing failure can result in a civil penalty of up to $150,000. A knowing penalty can result in a civil penalty up to $1,000,000. A failure to report also includes not reporting in a timely manner, accurately, or completely.

Ruth E. Granfors, a partner in the firm of Kirkpatrick & Lockhart LLP, has more than thirty years of legal experience practicing exclusively in the field of health care law, including ten years as counsel to the Pennsylvania Department of Health. Ms. Granfors represents a variety of health care providers in regulatory, health care enforcement, and insurance matters, including Medicare, Medicaid and privacy compliance; adverse licensing and government reimbursement decisions; government payment audits; and insurance plan disputes. She also advises clients on regulatory compliance in health care mergers, acquisitions, and reorganizations.

A Guide to Understanding the Impact of Health Care Reform on Employer Group Health Plans

Evelyn S. Traub

Partner

Troutman Sanders LLP

ASPATORE

Introduction

An employee benefits practice used to consist primarily of tax qualified retirement plans and executive compensation with almost no involvement with employer health and welfare plans. Sure, ERISA[1] applied to them but, for the most part, the details were left to the insurance agents and insurance carriers. While the non-discrimination rules applicable to self-funded group health plans required some attention, employers, even large ones, did not engage attorneys on an ongoing basis in matters relating to group health plans. That is no longer the case. The legal landscape has changed dramatically and employers now need all the help they can get.

Beginning with the passage of the Consolidated Omnibus Budget Reconciliation Act of 1985 (COBRA),[2] the Family and Medical Leave Act of 1993 (FMLA),[3] the Uniformed Services Employment and Reemployment Rights Act of 1994 (USERRA),[4] requirements relating to medical child support orders and Medicaid assignment provisions; the Newborns' and Mothers' Health Protection Act of 1996,[5] and the Mental Health Parity Act of 1998,[6] an employer's health plan compliance checklist started to grow. Then came the Health Insurance Portability and Accountability Act of 1996 (HIPAA).[7] HIPAA imposes portability requirements, notice requirements, privacy and security requirements, and coverage requirements. The employer's health plan compliance checklist expanded to include tasks that no longer could all be handled by the carrier or agent. Employer involvement with the legal compliance of their group health plans grew, especially for self-funded plans of large employers. With the Women's Health and Cancer Rights Act of 1998,[8] special ERISA claims procedures for different types of

---

[1] Employee Retirement Income Security Act of 1974, Pub. L. No. 93-406, 88 Stat. 829.
[2] Consolidated Omnibus Budget Reconciliation Act of 1985, Pub. L. No. 99-272, 100 Stat. 82.
[3] Family and Medical Leave Act of 1993, Pub. L. No. 103-3, 107 Stat. 6.
[4] Uniformed Services Employment and Reemployment Rights Act of 1994, Pub. L. No. 103-353, 108 Stat. 3149.
[5] Newborns' and Mothers' Health Protection Act of 1996, Pub. L. No. 104-204, 110 Stat. 2935.
[6] Mental Health Parity Act of 1996, Pub. L. No. 104-204, 110 Stat. 2944.
[7] Health Insurance Portability and Accountability Act of 1996, Pub. L. No. 104-191, 110 Stat. 1936.
[8] Women's Health and Cancer Rights Act of 1998, Pub. L. No. 105-277, 112 Stat. 2681-436.

health claims effective in 2002, the Paul Wellstone and Pete Domenici Mental Health Parity and Addiction Equity Act of 2008,[9] and the Genetic Information Nondiscrimination Act of 2008,[10] employers began to feel like the regulatory requirements were snowballing. Even a relatively small employer became subject to mounting compliance requirements, without the personnel and the expertise to confidently address them all.

In March 2010, the Patient Protection and Affordable Care Act (PPACA)[11] (referred to generally as health care reform) was passed. No business that touches the health care industry is unaffected. Insurance carriers, health care providers, and all employers must address various aspects of PPACA. For employers, the complexity has exploded. From plan coverage requirements for dependents and elimination of annual and lifetime limits, to mention a few that became effective for 2011, to the numerous reporting and disclosure requirements, employer shared responsibility requirements, and new taxes coming into effect at various times, employers are scrambling to understand it all and to structure their group health plans and their businesses to face the new world.

Looking at a compliance time line is perhaps the best checklist an employer can use to make sure that the various requirements are addressed. The provisions briefly described below are implemented through thousands of pages of regulations and "Frequently Asked Questions" (FAQs) issued by various government agencies. Many of the requirements present unique sets of challenges for employers. For the most part, the requirements described below do not apply to "excepted benefits" such as stand-alone dental or vision coverage, certain flexible spending arrangements, fixed indemnity coverage, and retiree coverage. Even determining whether a benefit is an excepted one can present interesting questions for an employer.

Grandfathered Status

To understand and implement the compliance timeline, one must first determine whether a plan has grandfathered status. To determine when

---

[9] Paul Wellstone and Pete Domenici Mental Health Parity and Addiction Equity Act of 2008, Pub. L. No. 110-343, 122 Stat. 3881.

[10] Genetic Information Nondiscrimination Act of 2008, Pub. L. No. 110-233, 122 Stat. 881.

[11] Patient Protection and Affordable Care Act, Pub. L. No. 111-148, 124 Stat. 119 (2010).

certain provisions of the health care reform apply, an employer must first determine whether its plan is "grandfathered." A grandfathered plan is one that was in existence on the date of enactment of health care reform, March 23, 2010. The following changes in a group health plan or health insurance coverage will terminate the grandfathered status of a plan:

- Eliminating all or substantially all benefits to diagnose or treat a particular condition;
- Increasing a percentage cost-sharing requirement (such as coinsurance) above the March 23, 2010 level. As an example, a change in the level of coinsurance from 20 percent to 25 percent for a particular type of service causes the plan to lose grandfathered status;
- Increasing fixed-amount cost-sharing requirements other than co-payments, such as a $500 deductible or a $2,500 out-of-pocket limit, by a total percentage measured from March 23, 2010 that is more than the sum of medical inflation and 15 percent;
- Increasing co-payments by an amount that exceeds the greater of:

  o A total percentage measured from March 23, 2010 that is more than the sum of medical inflation plus 15 percent, or
  o $5.00 increased by medical inflation as measured from March 23, 2010.

- Decreasing the employer's contribution rate toward any tier of coverage for any class of similarly situated individuals by more than 5 percent below the contribution rate on March 23, 2010.

In addition, a plan that takes the position that it is grandfathered must maintain records documenting the terms of the plan in effect on March 23, 2010, and any documents necessary to verify, clarify, or explain grandfathered status. These retained records must be kept for as long as the plan relies on its grandfathered status and must be made available for examination by participants, beneficiaries, and federal and state agencies upon request.

Once grandfathered status is lost, it may not be regained, and all the provisions of health care reform that apply to non-grandfathered plans will become applicable.

Compliance Timeline

Effective for Plan Years Beginning on or After September 23, 2010 (January 1, 2011 for Calendar Year Plans)

For All Plans Including Grandfathered Plans:

- *Prohibitions on lifetime limits and restrictions on annual limits.* Group health plans are generally prohibited from imposing lifetime limits on the dollar value of "essential health benefits." Essential health benefits include at least the following general categories and the items and services covered within the categories: ambulatory patient services; emergency services; hospitalization; maternity and newborn care; mental health and substance use disorder services, including behavioral health treatment; prescription drugs; rehabilitative services and devices; laboratory services; preventive and wellness services and chronic disease management; and pediatric services, including oral and vision care. A plan may impose lifetime dollar limits on specific covered benefits that are not essential health benefits and may apply per visit limitations. In addition, a plan is permitted to exclude all benefits for specific conditions. The maximum annual limits that may be imposed between 2011 and 2014 are restricted to no more than a phased in amount between $750,000 and $2 million. The restricted annual limits were waived for certain "limited benefit" or "mini-med" plans often offered to lower wage, part-time, or temporary workers or volunteers and stand-alone health reimbursement accounts (HRAs) through the 2013 plan year.

- *Dependent coverage for adult dependents.* Group health plans that provide dependent coverage must allow coverage for dependents (whether or not married) until the dependent turns twenty-six. Children of these adult dependents need not be covered unless the plan otherwise covers a participant's grandchild. This rule even applies to "grandfathered plans," except that adult dependent coverage is not required through December 31, 2013 if the adult dependent is eligible for coverage under another employer-sponsored group health plan.

- *No preexisting condition limit for children under nineteen.* Group health plans may not impose preexisting condition limitations on children under the age of nineteen. Under the Health Insurance Portability and Accountability Act (HIPAA),[12] a *group health plan* could exclude coverage for preexisting conditions generally for up to twelve months. However, the period of limitation was required to be reduced for an individual's prior creditable coverage (as long as that coverage did not end prior to sixty-three days before the enrollment date in the employer's plans.) Beginning in 2014, preexisting condition limitations must be eliminated for adults as well. Until 2014, the HIPAA rules continue to apply to all except children under the age of nineteen.

- *Prohibition on rescission of coverage.* Group health plans must not rescind coverage retroactively unless an individual commits fraud or makes an intentional misrepresentation of material fact. The most important impact of this rule is that plans cannot rescind coverage on the basis of inadvertent misstatements on coverage applications. In addition, if the plan wishes to exercise the right to rescind coverage for fraud or misrepresentation, the plan document must specifically provide for this action. To rescind coverage, plans must provide at least thirty days advance written notice to each participant who would be affected before coverage may be rescinded, thus affording the affected person or group time to contest the rescission or locate other coverage. A decision to rescind coverage is treated as an adverse benefit determination and subject to the ERISA claims and appeals process, including external review. The regulations do not restrict the ability to terminate coverage prospectively. In addition, retroactive cancellation or discontinuance of coverage will not violate the rules to the extent it is attributable to a failure to timely pay required premiums or contributions toward the cost of coverage.

For Non-Grandfathered Plans

- *Required coverage of preventive care and immunizations without cost sharing.* Non-grandfathered plans are required to cover preventive services and immunizations free of charge to the participants. Preventive services are defined by reference to published health recommendations and guidelines from:

---

[12] Health Insurance Portability and Accountability Act, Pub. L. No. 104-191, 110 Stat. 1936 (1996).

1. The United States Preventive Services Task Force,[13]
2. The Centers for Disease Control and Prevention Advisory Committee on Immunization Practices,[14] and
3. The Health Resources and Services Administration.[15]

The list is updated on an ongoing basis.[16] Plan sponsors should review the list carefully as there are services required to be provided at no cost that might not otherwise be covered by the health plan or included in the scope of preventive services, such as:

o Intensive behavioral counseling and intervention for weight and obesity issues;
o Intensive behavioral dietary counseling for adult patients with known risk factors for cardiovascular and diet-related chronic disease, delivered by primary care clinicians or by referral to other specialists, such as nutritionists or dietitians;
o Screening and behavioral counseling interventions to reduce alcohol misuse;
o Screening for depression in adults and major depressive disorders in adolescents;
o Tobacco cessation intervention; and
o All forms of FDA approved birth control.

• *Revamped intern appeals process and an external review process.* Group health plans must satisfy new requirements in addition to those set forth in the existing ERISA claims procedures. A plan cannot reduce or terminate a course of treatment without advance notice and opportunity for advance review. Individuals in urgent care situations receiving ongoing treatment must be allowed to proceed with expedited external review at the same time as the internal appeals process while continuing treatment. Failure to strictly

---

[13] *Recommendations*, U.S. PREVENTIVE SERVICES TASK FORCE, http://www.uspreventive servicestaskforce.org/recommendations.htm (last updated Dec. 2010).
[14] *Comprehensive Recommendations*, CDC, http://www.cdc.gov/vaccines/hcp/acip-recs/recs-comprehensive.html (last updated July 16, 2013).
[15] *Women's Preventive Service Guidelines*, HRSA, http://www.hrsa.gov/womensguidelines/.
[16] For a current list *see Preventive Services Covered Under the Affordable Care Act*, HHS.GOV/HEALTHCARE, http://www.hhs.gov/healthcare/facts/factsheets/2010/07/ prevent ive-services-list.html (last updated Sept. 27, 2012).

adhere to the requirements of the internal claims and appeals process will result in the claimant being deemed to have exhausted the internal claims and appeals process. Accordingly, the claimant may initiate an external review and pursue judicial review. This provision overturns language in the existing ERISA claims procedures and case law that had held that a health plan's substantial compliance with the claims review procedure prevented a claimant from being deemed to have exhausted the internal claims process. Plans, including self-insured plans, must comply with either a state external review process or the new federal external review process for determinations that involve medical judgment, such as medical necessity and whether a treatment is experimental or investigational, and rescission of coverage. In the case of a fully insured plan, the issuer is subject to the applicable external review requirements, so the fully insured health plan itself is not required to separately comply.

- *Prohibition on requiring prior authorization or increased cost sharing for emergency services.* Group health plans that cover emergency services must do so without the participant or health care provider having to obtain prior authorization and without regard to whether the health care provider furnishing the emergency services is an in-network provider. If a plan has network providers that provide benefits for emergency services, the plan may not impose any administrative requirement or limitation on benefits for out-of-network emergency services that are more restrictive than the requirements or limitations that apply to in-network emergency services. In addition, cost-sharing requirements imposed for out-of-network emergency services that are expressed as a co-payment amount or a coinsurance rate cannot exceed the cost-sharing requirements that would be imposed if the services were performed in-network. The restriction on cost-sharing does not preclude "balance billing" by an out-of-network provider for the difference between the cost of the services and the amounts received from the plan and the patient in the form of the co-payment or coinsurance amount. However, the plan cannot pay an unreasonably low amount to a provider, thus increasing the amount of the balance-bill. The plan's payment must be based on certain standard charges. These rules only apply to services provided in connection with an emergency medical condition.

They do not apply to services rendered in an emergency room for non-emergency conditions.

- *Prohibition on requiring authorization or referral for OB-GYN services.* If a group health plan provides coverage for obstetrical or gynecological care and requires or provides for the designation of a primary care provider, the plan may not require authorization or referral by the plan or any person (including a primary care provider) for a female participant who seeks obstetrical or gynecological care provided by an in-network health care professional who specializes in obstetrics or gynecology. The plan may, however, require the health care professional to agree to otherwise adhere to the plan's procedures regarding referrals and obtaining prior authorization and providing services pursuant to a treatment plan approved by the plan.

- *Requirement that enrollees be able to select a primary care provider or pediatrician from any available primary care provider that is accepting new patients.* If a group health plan requires or provides for a participant to make a primary care provider designation, the plan must permit the participant to designate any primary care provider who is available to accept the participant and who participates in the network. In addition, if a plan requires or provides for a participant to designate a primary care provider for a child, the plan must permit the designation of any physician who specializes in pediatrics as the child's primary care provider as long as the provider participates in the network and is available to accept the child.

Special Notice Requirements

Adult Children and Those Excluded Based on Lifetime Limit

Written notice of the right to enroll must be provided to adult children and individuals who previously reached a plan's lifetime limit and are otherwise still eligible under the plan. The Department of Labor published model notices for these special enrollment events.[17] This was a onetime notice given in open enrollments for the first plan year beginning after September 23, 2010.

---

[17] *See Extension of Care for adult Children*, U.S. DEP'T. LAB., http://www.dol.gov/ ebsa/healthreform/regulations/extensionofcoverage.html; *see also Preexisting Condition*

Choice of Health Care Professionals

Participants must be provided notice of their right to—

1. Choose a primary care provider or a pediatrician when a plan requires designation of a primary care physician; and
2. Obtain obstetrical or gynecological care without prior authorization. This is an ongoing requirement and must be provided whenever a summary plan description or other similar description of plan benefits is provided to a participant or beneficiary. The Department of Labor published the Model Notice on Patient Protections that can be used to satisfy the notice requirement.[18]

Grandfathered Status

To maintain grandfathered status, a plan or health insurance coverage must include in any plan material provided to the participant or beneficiary describing the benefits under the plan and a statement that the plan believes it is a grandfathered health plan, and provide contact information for questions and complaints. The regulations provide model language that can be used for this purpose.[19] As long as the plan intends to maintain grandfathered status, this is an ongoing requirement and must be provided whenever summary plan benefits are provided to a participant or beneficiary.

Effective for Plans Years Beginning on or After January 1, 2011

No Reimbursement for Over-the-Counter Drugs

Expenses incurred for over-the-counter drugs are not eligible for reimbursement through medical flexible spending accounts or health reimbursement accounts. This rule does not apply if the over-the-counter drug is prescribed by a physician or is insulin.

Exclusions, Lifetime and Annual Limits, Rescissions, and Patient Protections, U.S. DEP'T. LAB., http://www.dol.gov/ebsa/healthreform/regulations/ preexistingconditionexclusions.html.

[18] *See Preexisting Condition Exclusions, Lifetime and Annual Limits, Rescissions, and Patient Protections, supra* note 14.

[19] *See* Grandfathered Health Plans, U.S. DEP'T. LAB., http://www.dol.gov/ebsa/health reform/regulations/grandfatheredhealthplans.html.

Effective for Plan Years Beginning on or After January 1, 2012

Reporting the Value of Group Health Coverage on Form W-2s

All employers are required to report the aggregate cost (the total amount paid by both the employer and employee) of applicable employer-sponsored group health plan coverage on only those employees' Form W-2s who were enrolled in a health plan coverage during the year reported.

Employers who issued less than 250 Form W-2s in 2011 are exempt until further guidance is issued. The value of group health plans is being reported for informational purposes only as a source for comparable consumer information on the cost of health care coverage. The value is not to be included in the employee's income and is not subject to federal taxation.

Beginning September 23, 2012

Summary of Benefits and Coverage (SBC)

Beginning September 23, 2012, health insurers and self-insured group health plans are required to provide SBCs, free of charge, to all individuals enrolling in health coverage. The purpose of the SBC is to provide individuals with standard information so they can compare medical plans as they make decisions about which plan to choose. The SBC must contain specific information and be presented in a uniform format, using terminology understandable by the average plan enrollee, not exceeding four double-sided pages in at least 12-point font.

The SBC may be provided either as a stand-alone document or in combination with other summary materials (for example, a summary plan description) if the SBC information is intact and prominently displayed at the beginning of the materials (such as immediately after the table of contents in a summary plan description) and provided in accordance with the delivery timing requirements for the SBC. The specific format is available on the DOL website and is updated from time to time.[20]

---

[20] *See Summary of Benefits and Coverage and Uniform Glossary*, U.S. DEP'T. LAB., http://www.dol.gov/ebsa/healthreform/regulations/summaryofbenefits.html.

Advance Notice Requirement

Also beginning September 23, 2012, if a group health plan or health insurance issuer makes any material modification in any of the terms of the plan or coverage involved that is not reflected in the most recently provided SBC, the plan or issuer must provide notice of the modification to enrollees not later than sixty days prior to the date on which such modification becomes effective. This means that a revised SBC must be issued if there are mid-year material changes to the terms of a plan or coverage. Material changes that are effective in a new plan year must be described in the SBCs issued during open enrollment.

For Plan Years Beginning on or After January 1, 2013

Contributions to FSAs Limited

Contributions to medical flexible spending accounts by plan participants will be limited to $2,500 per year. Contributions by the employer and any permitted carryover are not counted toward this $2,500 limit.

October 1, 2013 and Ongoing

Exchange Notice

Employers must provide to each of their employees as of October 1, 2013, and to all new employees at the time of hiring within fourteen days after an employee's start date, a written notice informing the employees of the existence of the government-run health care exchanges. If the employer's group health plan's share of the total allowed costs of benefits provided under the plan is less than 60 percent of such costs, employees may be eligible for a premium tax credit if they purchase a qualified health plan through an exchange.

If employees purchase a qualified health plan through an exchange, they may lose the employer contribution (if any) to any group health plan the employer offers. All or a portion of this contribution may be excluded from income for federal income tax purposes. To satisfy these content requirements, model language is available from the DOL.

For Plan Years Ending on or After October 1, 2012

Patient-Centered Outcomes Research Institute (PCORI) Fees

Health care reform established the Patient-Centered Outcomes Research Trust Fund, a nonprofit corporation that will research clinical effectiveness, risks, and benefits of medical treatments, services, procedures, drugs, and other strategies that treat, manage, diagnose, or prevent illness or injury, and which will be funded by Patient-Centered Outcomes Research Institute (PCORI) fees. The fee will be imposed on health insurance policies and self-insured health plans. The amount of the fee is $2.00 ($1.00 in the case of plan years ending before Oct. 1, 2013) multiplied by the average number of lives covered under each plan or policy. Because the fee is based on the covered lives, not just the number of employees or plan participants, there are special rules for determining the number used in the PCORI fee calculation if an exact number is not available. The fee is imposed on issuers of health insurance policies and plan sponsors of applicable self-insured plans for each policy/plan year ending on or after October 1, 2012 and before October 1, 2019. All plan sponsors and insurers will be required to pay the fee by July 31 of the calendar year following the last day of the plan year using the Form 720 (Quarterly Excise Tax Return). For a calendar year plan, the first PCORI fee was due for the 2012 calendar year on July 31, 2013.

For Plan Years Beginning on or After January 1, 2014

Preexisting Condition Exclusions

Group health plans are no longer permitted to impose limitations on coverage for preexisting conditions on any plan participant. This prohibition took effect earlier—as of plan years beginning on or after September 23, 2010—with respect to individuals who are under nineteen years of age.

Exclusion of Adult Children

Grandfathered plans are no longer permitted to exclude adult children who have health care coverage under the child's employer's plan.

Waiting Periods Limited

A group health plan may not apply any waiting period that exceeds ninety days. A waiting period is defined as the period of time that must pass before coverage for an employee or dependent who is otherwise eligible to enroll under the terms of the plan can become effective. For this purpose, being eligible for coverage means the individual has met the plan's substantive eligibility conditions (such as being in an eligible job classification or achieving job-related licensure requirements specified in the plan's terms). This means that other coverage conditions are generally permitted, unless the condition is designed to avoid compliance with the ninety-day waiting period limitation. If an employee is permitted to elect coverage that will begin on a date that does not exceed the ninety-day waiting period limitation, then the ninety-day waiting period limitation is considered satisfied. In other words, it is not a violation merely because employees take additional time to elect coverage. However, a requirement that an employee successfully complete a reasonable and bona fide employment-based orientation period may be imposed as a condition of coverage, thus briefly delaying the beginning of the ninety-day waiting period and enabling the employer to enroll employees on the first day of a month. The current proposed regulations suggest one month as the maximum length of the orientation period. It is unclear what steps an employer needs to take to adopt an orientation period.

Annual Dollar Limits

The restrictions on the amount of the annual limits on the dollar amount of "essential health benefits" for any individual are replaced with a prohibition on such limits. Essential health benefits include ambulatory care; emergency care; hospitalization; maternity/newborn; mental health and substance use disorder services, including behavioral health treatment; prescription drugs; rehabilitative and habilitative services and devises; lab; preventive/wellness and chronic disease management; and pediatric services including dental and vision care. The temporary waiver on the annual limit rule expires. This means that "limited benefit" or "mini-med" plans often offered to lower wage, part-time, or temporary workers or volunteers and stand-alone health reimbursement accounts (HRAs) cannot be maintained after the 2013 plan year. Retiree-only HRAs are still permitted. In addition, HRAs that are integrated with other coverage as part of a larger group health plan are permitted. The other coverage referred to may include the group health plan of a different employer.

Coverage for Certain Clinical Trials

Non-grandfathered plans must provide coverage for certain clinical trials involving cancer and other life-threatening conditions and cannot deny or limit coverage of routine patient costs for items and services furnished in connection with the trial, or discriminate against an individual based on participation in the trial.

Essential Health Benefits

Non-grandfathered, fully insured, small group plans must provide essential health benefits. Under an extension announced in November 2013, states may permit insurance carriers to renew policies that do not meet these requirements during a specific transition period.

Cost Sharing

Cost sharing provisions in non-grandfathered plans may not exceed high deductible health plan (HDHP) maximum out-of-pocket limits. For 2014 these maximums are $6,350 for self-only coverage and $12,700 for family coverage. For 2015 these maximums are $6,600 for self-only coverage and $13,200 for family coverage. If a plan uses multiple providers, such as a separate pharmacy benefit manager or behavioral health management organization, a one-year safe harbor extension applies if certain conditions are met. Health savings account, flexible spending account, and health reimbursement account contributions may be taken into account as regulations permit.

Reinsurance Fees

A transitional reinsurance fee is imposed in the calendar years 2014, 2015, and 2016 to collect approximately $10 billion in 2014; $6 billion in 2015; and $4 billion in 2016. Health insurance issuers of fully insured policies and sponsors of self-insured plans are liable for the fee. The reinsurance fee is calculated by multiplying the number of "covered lives" by the "contribution rate" for the calendar year for all covered plans. Because the fee is based on the covered lives, not just the number of employees or plan participants, there are special rules for determining the number used in the transition reinsurance fee calculation if an exact number is not available. Plan sponsors of self-funded plans and health insurance carriers will submit plan enrollment information to HHS by November 15, 2014. Within fifteen days of that submission, HHS will notify the employer/insurer of the amount that must be paid as a reinsurance fee. The employer/insurer then has thirty days to pay the fee, which means that employers generally will pay the first reinsurance fee by the end of 2014.

For Plan Years Beginning on or After January 1, 2015

Employer Shared Responsibility Requirements

Generally employers with more than fifty employees will be required to offer group health coverage or pay a penalty of up to $2,000 per full-time employee. On July 9, 2013, the various agencies charged with enforcing PPACA announced that compliance with the employer responsibility rules would be postponed from 2014 to 2015. On February 10, 2014, an additional extension was announced for compliance with the employer responsibility rules for employers with between fifty and ninety-nine employees until 2016.

Applicable Large Employer

An employer that employed an average of fifty (one hundred in the case of 2015) or more combined full-time employees and full-time equivalent (FTE) employees during the prior calendar year will be considered an "applicable large employer" and subject to the share responsibility provisions.

The definition of an applicable large employer requires that all full-time employees (i.e., employees who work at least thirty hours per week, or 130 hours per month) and the full-time equivalent employees (rounded to the next lower whole number) be added together to determine if the total is fifty or more. The determination of applicable larger employer status is made on a controlled group basis.

The calculation is done on a monthly basis as follows:

- Determine the number of hours worked by each employee in each calendar month;
- Determine the number of employees who average thirty or more hours per week in each calendar month;
- Add up all the employees who averaged thirty hours or more for all the twelve months;
- For the rest of the employees add up all the hours they worked in each calendar month (do not count more than 120 hours), then divide by 120. The result is the full-time equivalents.
- Add the full-time equivalents to the employees that averaged more than thirty hours per week; and
- Divide the grand total by twelve.

If the result is fifty or more (one hundred in the case of 2015), the employer is an applicable large employer for the following calendar year. This test is done each year for the upcoming calendar year. For 2015, the employer will be an applicable larger employer if the one hundred-employee threshold is exceeded in 2014. The proposed regulations allow for a transitional rule in 2014 under which the determination may be made based on any consecutive six-month period in 2014 (as opposed to the whole calendar year) to determine the employer's status for 2015.

In addition, an exception applies if an employer is an applicable large employer solely because of a large number of seasonal employees. The seasonal employer exception provides that an employer is not considered to be an applicable larger employer if the sum of the full-time employees and full-time equivalent employees exceeds fifty for 120 days or less (or four months or less) during the preceding calendar year.

The determination of a new employer's status as an applicable large employer is based on the employer's reasonable expectations.

<u>Choice Between Offering Coverage or Paying Penalty Tax</u>

If an employer who qualifies as an applicable large employer does not provide the type of health care coverage described below, the employer may be subject to tax penalties. If the employer fails to offer the coverage for any day in the month during which the full-time employee was employed, the coverage is not considered to have been offered. If the employee terminates employment, coverage is considered offered for the month if it would have been available every day of the month had the employee continued employment for the entire month. It is not required that the employee accept coverage to be treated as having been offered the coverage. An employer is not required to provide coverage if the employee fails to pay his or her share of the premium. A grace period for payment similar to the grace period for the payment of COBRA premiums will apply. Coverage will generally be considered offered to an employee only if it is also offered to the employee's dependents. Dependents, for purposes of the penalty, are generally defined as an employee's child who is under twenty-six years of age. There is no requirement that an employer offer coverage to an employee's spouse, step children, or foster children.

The penalty generally is applied separately to each member of the controlled group. While applicable large employer status is determined on an aggregated basis, each member is treated as a separate entity for purposes of determining liability for, and the amount of, any penalty. Thus, for example, an employer who is a member of a controlled group of an applicable large employer that does not offer coverage will be subject to a penalty based on the number of its own full-time employees and not on the number of full-time employees employed by the entire control group. The thirty (eighty for 2015) employee reduction applies only once to a controlled group and is spread ratably among the members of the group. For pass-through entities such as partnerships and S corporations, the penalty is applied at the entity level and does not pass though to the owners.

Offer of Coverage

To avoid potential tax penalties, an employer that is an applicable large employer must provide its full-time employees (and their dependents) with the opportunity to enroll in coverage that

1. Qualifies as "minimum essential coverage,"
2. Is "affordable," and
3. Provides a "minimum value."

This coverage is referred to as "qualified health care coverage." If the employer does not provide qualified health care coverage *and* at least one full-time employee has enrolled in a health plan through an Exchange for which a tax credit or cost-sharing subsidy is allowed or paid, the employer will be subject to a penalty. Only full-time employees (and their dependents) are required to be offered qualified health care coverage to avoid the potential penalty. Any employee who is not considered a full-time employee as described below may be excluded from coverage.

Determination of Full-Time Status

For this purpose, a full-time employee is an employee who is employed on an average of at least thirty hours of service per week, or 130 hours of service in a calendar month. Hours of service include each hour for which an employee is paid (or entitled to payment), and each hour for which an employee is paid or entitled to be paid on account of a period during which the employee does not perform any duties due to vacation, holiday, illness, disability, layoff, jury duty, military leave, or leave of absence. Hours of service do not include hours of service worked outside the United States. Determining hours of service and full-time status is the subject of a complex regulatory scheme requiring that records be maintained which an employer perhaps had not maintained previously.

The employer must determine hours for non-hourly employees, determine full-time status for current and ongoing employees, determine full-time status for new employees who are reasonably expected to work full-time and for those whose hours may be variable or seasonal, transition new employees into ongoing employees, establish measurement periods for making these status determinations, and address mid-year changes in status, breaks in service, and unpaid time.

This tracking and recordkeeping is perhaps the most challenging provision of PPACA[21] for employers. Even though the shared responsibility rules do not apply until 2015, identifying measurement periods and tracking hours must begin well in advance, even as early as October 2013, to use the longest available measurement periods.

---

[21] Patient Protection and Affordable Care Act, Pub. L. No. 111-148, 124 Stat. 119 (2010).

Minimum Essential Coverage

Minimum essential coverage is an employer-sponsored group health plan (but would not include a stand-alone dental or vision plan, for example). Unlike the insurance provisions for small group employers (see above), there is no requirement that any particular services be covered and there are no other detailed coverage requirements (other than those previously outlined.)

Affordability

Coverage is "affordable" if the employee's required contribution toward the annual premiums for *employee-only* coverage under the plan for the least expensive tier of coverage does not exceed 9.5 percent of the employee's household income. Given that employers may not know an employee's household income, for purposes of avoiding the employer tax penalty, the IRS has provided three safe harbors:

- *W-2.* The first safe harbor allows an employer to treat the coverage as affordable if the employer's required contributions do not exceed 9.5 percent of the employee's Box 1 W-2 wages. This safe harbor is of little use because it is based on the W-2 wages for the year at issue; that cannot be known for certain until the year is over. It also includes pre-tax contributions toward 401(k) plans and pre-tax premium payments.
- *Rate of Pay.* Under the rate of pay safe harbor, affordability is based on a salaried employee's monthly salary, and, for an hourly employee, the hourly rate of pay times 130 hours per month. The rate of pay safe harbor can only be used if the employee's pay does not decrease during the year.
- *Federal Poverty Line.* Under the federal poverty line safe harbor, affordability is based on the federal poverty level for a single individual. For 2014, the federal poverty line for a single individual is $11,670 per year and $23,850 for a family of four. This level is adjusted annually in January.

Minimum Value

Coverage provides a minimum value if the plan's share of total allowed costs of benefits provided is at least 60 percent of the total costs. Generally, this means that the plan may not shift more than 40 percent of the overall covered expenses (such as co-pays, deductibles, and coinsurance) to participants. The agencies in charge of health care reform have issued guidance on how to calculate minimum value.[22] Typically, the insurance company for a fully insured plan will be able to tell the employer if the plan meets the minimum value requirement.

Employer Penalties

No Coverage

If in any month, an applicable large employer does not offer *any* employer-sponsored group health plan to 70 percent of its full-time employees (and their dependents) in 2015 or 95 percent in later years, the employer may be subject to a non-deductible penalty for such month. This penalty, referred to as the $2,000 penalty, is $166.67 per month or $2,000 per year. The penalty will apply only if at least one of the full-time employees enrolls in one of the government-sponsored exchanges *and* is eligible for a subsidy or tax credit to pay for the coverage obtained through the Exchange.

For each such month, the penalty is equal to (a) the total number of full-time employees in excess of eighty for 2015 and thirty thereafter during the month, multiplied by (b) $166.67. For example, if the employer employed 110 full-time employees in 2015 and did not provide any group health coverage, and any full-time employee obtained coverage through an exchange and received a subsidy, the penalty would be $5,000.10 per month—(100-80) x $166.67—$60,001.20 per year. The penalty amount may be increased from year to year.

Coverage Not "Affordable" or of "Minimum Value"

If in any month, an applicable large employer offers a group health plan, but the plan either (a) is not "affordable" or (b) does not provide "minimum value," the employer may be subject to a penalty for that month. This penalty, referred to as the $3,000 penalty, is $250 per month

---

[22] *See* Department of Health and Human Services, *Minimum Value Calculator Methodology*, CMS.GOV, *available at* http://www.cms.gov/CCIIO/Resources/ Regulations-and-Guidance/Downloads/mv-calculator-methodology.pdf.

or $3,000 per year. The penalty will apply if at least one of the full-time employees enrolls in one of the government-sponsored exchanges and is eligible for a subsidy or tax credit to pay for the coverage obtained through the exchange. For each such month, the penalty is equal to (a) the total number of full-time employees who enrolled in coverage under the exchange *and* were eligible for the subsidy or tax credit during the month, multiplied by (b) $250.00. However, the penalty is capped at the penalty that would have applied if the employer did not offer coverage through any group health plan to any full-time employee.

An employee is eligible for a subsidy or tax credit if his or her household income is between 100 percent and 400 percent of the federal poverty line. For 2014, this means more than $11,670 and less than $46,680 for a single individual and more than $23,850 and less than $95,400 for a family of four. The level is adjusted annually in January. For example in 2016, assume an employer employs sixty full-time employees and provides group health coverage that is not "affordable" with respect to twenty-seven employees who then obtain coverage through an exchange and receive a subsidy. The monthly penalty would normally be $6,750 (27 x $250.00). However, the monthly penalty is capped at the penalty that would apply if no coverage had been offered to any full-time employees—which is (60-30) x $166.67 = $5,000.10.

Effective of *de minimis* Rule

An employer is not subject to the $2,000 penalty if it offers minimum affordance coverage to at least 70 percent of its full-time employees in 2015 and 95 percent in later years. However, the employer may still be subject to the $3,000 penalty with respect to employees in the 30 percent/5 percent of full-time employees who did not receive the offer of coverage if such employee enrolls in coverage under the exchange *and* were eligible for the subsidy or tax credit.

Employer Reporting

Reporting for Compliance with Applicable Large Employer Rules

An employer that is subject to the shared responsibility rules must report certain information to the IRS following the end of a calendar year. A separate Form 1095-C[23] is prepared with respect to each full-time employee and the Forms 1095-C are transmitted to the IRS using a Form 1094-C, similar to the way an employer transmits the separate Forms W-2 prepared for each employee using a Form W-3. The Forms 1095-C will also be provided to the full-time employees, similar to a Form W-2, to substantiate his or her coverage to obtain relief from the individual penalty applicable to all individuals who do not maintain health insurance. The deadlines for furnishing the Forms 1095-C to participants is January 31 following the end of the calendar year, the same date as the Form W-2. The deadline for furnishing the report to the IRS is February 28, or March 31 if filing electronically, the same as the Form W-3.

The IRS has provided alternative methods for complying with the reporting requirements. Simplified reporting may be available for an employer that provides an offer of employee-only coverage at a cost to the employee of no more than 9.5 percent of the federal poverty level for the entire year. The general reporting is required for employees who received the offer of described coverage for less than twelve months. Solely for 2015, an employer that offers employee-only coverage at a cost to the employee of no more than 9.5 percent of the federal poverty level to at least 95 percent of its full-time employees may be able to take advantage of simplified reporting even if the offer of coverage was not for the entire year. In addition, if an employer certifies that it offers coverage to at least 98 percent of its full-time employees at an employee-only cost that is affordable under any of the IRS safe harbors, the employer is not required to identify or specify the number of full-time employees. However, the employer must still report the required information to the employee.

Reporting to Verify Individual Eligibility for Subsidies and Credits

The providers of minimum essential health coverage, such as insurers of self-funded group health plans, must report certain information to the IRS about the type and period of coverage. The information must also be furnished in statements to the covered individuals on a Form 1095-B. A separate Form 1095-B is prepared with respect to each full-time employee and the Forms

---

[23] Information Reporting of Minimum Essential Coverage, 79 Fed. Reg. 13,220, 13,224 (Mar. 10, 2014) (to be codified at 21 C.F.R. pts. 1, 301, 602).

1095-B are transmitted to the IRS using a Form 1094-B, similar to the way an employer transmits the separate Forms W-2 prepared for each employee using a Form W-3. A self-insured applicable large employer subject to the reporting described above can file a combined report (on a Form 1094-C) to satisfy the two reporting requirements. The deadlines for furnishing the Forms 1095-B to participants is January 31 following the end of the calendar year, the same date as the Form W-2. The deadline for furnishing the report to the IRS is February 28, or March 31 if filing electronically, the same as the Form W-3.

For Plan Years Beginning on or After January 1, 2016

Employer Shared Responsibility Requirements

Employers with between fifty and ninety-nine employees will be required to offer group health coverage or pay a penalty of up to $2,000 per full-time employee. In addition, the *de minimus* threshold for the applicable $2,000 penalty is raised to 95 percent of all full-time employees and the $2,000 penalty is determined based on full-time employees in excess of thirty, rather than eighty.

For Plan Years Beginning on or After January 1, 2018

Excise Taxes on "Cadillac" Plans

A 40 percent non-deductible excise tax will be imposed on the amount, if any, by which the monthly cost of an employee's employer-sponsored health coverage exceeds a threshold amount. Initially, the dollar amounts that are used to determine most employees' annual limits are $10,200 for self-only coverage and $27,500 for coverage other than self-only. These amounts are expected to be adjusted from time to time and may even increase before 2018 when the excise tax becomes effective.

Effective When Regulations Published

Automatic Enrollment

Employers with more than 200 employees will be required to automatically enroll employees into their lowest cost group health plans. Employees will be able to opt out of coverage.

Non-Discrimination Standards to Apply to Fully Insured Plans

In a major change from prior law, non-grandfathered, fully insured plans must meet non-discrimination standards similar to those imposed on self-insured health plans.

Both of these requirements will become effective after regulations are published describing the details of their application.

Conclusion

The explosion of rules and regulations surrounding employer group health care can be overwhelming. Focusing and understanding the requirements is a daunting task that requires organization, attention to detail, and a team approach. No one employee within an organization can fully grasp the complete scope; the assistance of professionals outside the employer's organization is almost a necessity. Attorneys should reach out to clients to find out what steps they have taken to comply with health care reform and help them identify additional actions that need to be taken and resources that need to be employed to ensure compliance and\or minimize the potential penalties.

An employee benefits practice is becoming more and more specialized. Mastering health care reform is as complex as executive compensation and tax qualified plans. In my view, employer group health plans are fast becoming a specialty practice in their own right.

Key Takeaways

- Use a compliance timeline to assist your clients in making sure they address all of the items required of them concerning their health plan.
- Take advantage of government websites and Frequently Asked Questions to find answers and focus your research.
- It is of utmost importance to first determine if the health plan in question has grandfathered status. If it does, the terms of the grandfathered plan must be documented as it was in effect on March 23, 2010, the date of the enactment of the health care reform.

- Be mindful of the compliance requirements that change from year to year, especially going forward.
- Encourage clients to ask for help when attempting to determine requirements applicable to its employer group health care plan and understand the complexities of the various rules. It is near impossible to do it alone.
- Encourage clients to start now to prepare for the employer shared responsibilities rules.

Evelyn S. Traub is a partner in Troutman Sanders LLP's Employee Benefits and Executive Compensation Practice. She is the section leader of the firm's Tax and Benefits Section. Her practice is focused on advising public, private and governmental employers on ERISA, tax and related aspects of health and welfare benefits, flexible compensation, cafeteria plans, executive compensation, and tax-qualified plans.

Mrs. Traub received her JD from University of Richmond and her LLM in taxation from Georgetown University. She also has a BS in business administration from the University of Richmond where she graduated cum laude in 1977. She has been listed in Best Lawyers in America in Employee Benefits (ERISA) Law since 2001.

Mrs. Traub is a frequent speaker and author on employee benefits topics.

Strategic Considerations in Designing and Implementing an Effective Corporate Compliance Program in the Health Care and Life Sciences Industry

Wendy C. Goldstein

Partner

Cooley LLP

ASPATORE

Introduction

The scope of my practice is very broad and includes regulatory, compliance, operational, and strategic counseling for clients in the traditional health care arena, all facets of the "life sciences" industry, and those who invest in such concerns. One significant development in the client base is that there have been many new entrants to this significant health care ecosystem. For example, technology companies, such companies defined broadly to include emerging companies and established players of all sizes, have become very active in innovating new products and platforms to deliver health care and life sciences items and services directly to consumers, providers, and payors.

A good way to visualize the transformation occurring in my regulatory practice is to draw three concentric circles representing health care companies, life science companies, and technology companies. The overlap represents the collaborations and interrelationships between the parties; the legal counseling is the shaded area as the regulatory and compliance topics/issues overlap. Today these three circles fall short of overlapping completely, but over time these players will intersect to an even greater degree than the current state.

This development is a significant and very positive advancement for the potential of expanding access to health care service and items, while potentially reducing the cost of delivery and improving quality. One only needs to look at the percentage of the GNP dedicated to health care to understand its impact on the United States economy. Creative solutions are mandatory to control expenditures. Among other developments, advances in technology are one answer to addressing escalating costs.

With the opportunities that the advances in technology create, health regulatory challenges emerge. Companies that have never been involved in a highly regulated area are confronting a myriad of regulatory parameters that have not yet been specifically addressed by the law.

I have been practicing for almost twenty years. To a certain extent, much of what is new was once old. This is especially true with shared risk arrangements and other reimbursement methodologies. While there may be a new innovative twist from time to time, many ideas grow on the past.

Many technology products are, in fact, new. One of the biggest regulatory challenges that we face is that science, technology, and the law are not necessarily moving at the same speed. When we provide counsel to certain clients, there is now, more than ever, unique regulatory analysis and compliance issues that must be addressed. In many instances, there are not many specifics to rely upon—as innovation is outpacing the law. In such instances, it is important to analogize and to be thinking about ways to work with the legislators and regulators to education and update the law.

The other part of my practice is to defend health care and life science companies in the event of a government investigation, a congressional inquiry, or another type of inquiry (no matter from where it emanates), as it relates to the sales, marketing, promotion, and clinical research of items or services that are reimbursed by federal health care programs. Providing all of these services to clients—strategic counseling, regulatory and compliance counseling, and staying current on policy, as well as defending these companies when needed—makes the practice very well rounded as it relates to companies operating and strategizing in this gray world.

The Role of the Affordable Care Act

Many aspects of the Affordable Care Act[1] have been implemented. For example, the health care exchanges offering essential health benefits are operating for consumers at the state and national level. There have been some delays with respect to implementation deadlines such as the employer mandates. Some very well-publicized technological issues in the implementation of the exchanges also occurred. Regulations continue to be promulgated. There also are outstanding questions with key items associated with the law. For example, some members of Congress question agency guidance on whether the essential health benefits packages are "federal health care programs" from a legal perspective. This question has significant regulatory ramifications.

Plans are testing the waters to see how the first year of participation is going to play out in terms of who is signing up in their specific plan, what the risk profile ultimately looks like, how the program moves forward, and whether their individual beneficiaries are ultimately going to stay with their products

---

[1] Patient Protection and Affordable Care Act, **Pub. L. No. 111-148**, 124 Stat. 119 **(2010).**

or others. As with any new product, a lot of assumptions went into how organizations put together their own packages, so there is going to be a great deal of experimentation and tinkering, based on, among other things, the practical and realistic lessons learned.

One very interesting development is that there are new players to the insurance market. In New York, for example, there are plans that are offering products on the exchanges that never existed before. Some of these new market entrants are innovative and using new technology to deliver certain health care services to enrollees. There is a recognized need to make health care services more accessible in all respects and these plans are working through the laws to create products that address this patient need. Some examples on the way in which the benefits are being offered include the use of more telemedicine, online schedule bookers, and other services to coordinate patient care. It will be interesting to see which companies are the "winners" and which are the "losers" in the new marketplace, wrought with hurdles. Traditional large players? New entrants? Co-ops? Others? Time will tell.

With respect to the compliance strategies for the plans themselves, as opposed to business partners, as mentioned above, there are still unresolved issues. However, compliance oversight and certifications of such is mandatory. Plans are not unfamiliar with these requirements. One really good analysis is Medicare Advantage, with and without the prescription drug plans. Payors who offer such plans are very familiar with the compliance infrastructure that needs to be implemented to offer their plans to the public and the required elements of an effective corporate compliance program. Some additional information and requirements do exist for exchange plans, however.

More significant challenges come into play with the business associates and the business partners of plans, such as manufacturers. For example, pharmaceutical manufacturers who offer products that will be part of a plan offered through an exchange. Are co-pay mitigation programs such as consumer coupons subject to federal health care anti-kickback law requirements? What about the other business partners to exchange plans such as some types of providers who adopt waivers of co-pay programs under certain scenarios? These all need to be analyzed and structured in consideration of such laws as the anti-kickback laws, and its relevant guidance including advisory letters, and other civil monetary penalty laws. The Affordable Care Act has presented the time to review and update all payor corporate compliance programs as well as the programs of their business partners.

Strategies

There are many different strategies with respect to working through corporate compliance issues in an evolving and uncertain environment. Strategically, it is imperative to stay on top of all guidance and have a nimble compliance plan that can adapt to changes quickly. With the pace of developments, there is often not time to consider the items for the next annual audit plan.

It also may be that the company needs to make strategic decisions that involve their risk tolerance in this environment. One item is for certain, compliance issues need to be considered on a case-by-case basis for each of the organizations. How it establishes a culture of compliance from the board through all ranks of its employees is critical. Also, how it interacts and contracts with business partners must be part of the dialogue. It is critical for health care and life science attorneys who provide compliance counsel to spend time with clients walking them through legal analyses, the state of the law and the guidances, and government and agency enforcement activity and positions. This is all critical for a client to conduct a risk analysis.

Unfortunately, legislative history is sometimes sparse where we need it. Open and frank dialogue is important with clients. When you are in the regulatory legal field, you are a student for life; it simply does not stop. In my specialty, we always have changes to the laws as our products and services go through the appropriations process annually. We also must pay close attention to the enforcement trends as we design and implement compliance plans.

The chief compliance officer is a tough position to fill. The job is a large one with critical skill set needs in many areas. Officers and directors must satisfy their fiduciary obligation by staying on top of compliance. They must ask questions and follow up regularly. These are two of the basic building blocks to an effective program, even in light of the uncertainty.

The Impact of the Sunshine Law

The Sunshine Law,[2] or physician and GPO transparency law, is a section of the Affordable Care Act that has been implemented. Although this legislation was included in the Affordable Care Act, it was stand-alone legislation for a number of years. Generally it requires the reporting of certain remuneration paid by manufacturers to health care professionals and academic medical centers in connection with different activities. It preempts some state law counterparts, but not all states depending on the scope of the state law. It is likely to have a spillover effect into other inquiries and enforcement. The Sunshine Law, among other things, is intended to provide the public insight into the financial relationship(s) between manufacturers and prescribers. It is intended to make relationships more transparent and to expose real or perceived conflicts of interest between the parties.

One of the most significant questions, as it relates to transparency, is how will the reports be used? Is it for consumers, is it for litigation, is it for government investigation, is it for public watch dogs, is it for all of the above, or is it for others? What effect will it have on the industry as it relates to these reportable relationships? Will providers act differently? What kind of conclusions can you really draw from this information? There are a lot of questions out there. There are always going to be questions with respect to the information that is reported because the investment in systems used to collect this data is such a huge expenditure. It takes a lot to develop a system to locate and collect the information that gets reported.

The concept of transparency in health care, as it relates to different relationships, not necessarily just between manufacturers and the health care professionals or the academic medical institutions, is a major trend. Whether Group Purchasing Organizations (GPOs), providers, pharmacies, researchers, nursing homes, more information is being made public through federal and state legislation annually. One question is how do you educate people with respect to using the data appropriately and putting the appropriate qualifications around the methodology for the collection?

---

[2] 42 U.S.C. § 1320a-7h (2012).

Important Case Law

We have seen many government settlements over the past several years in connection with *qui tam* actions under the False Claims Act,[3] as it relates to manufacturers and health care institutions. On the manufacturer side you get a sense of some of the relationships between and among the different parties that sell, promote, and purchase, and what could have gone awry. Civil settlements do not mean that there is an admission; there is only an admission when it is criminal. There are a whole host of recent settlements that have been both civil and criminal.

The scope of damages in recent settlements has eclipsed the billion dollar mark. In connection with Johnson & Johnson,[4] for example, with the alleged off-label promotion of certain products, the government had concerns regarding the financial incentives as to why certain products were prescribed over other products. It suggests that the financial incentives skewed the clinical judgment, and that is also why they were promoted. The cycle continued from back in 2003 with respect to misbranding, or off-label promotion, and also with respect to the concept of the relationship with the health care professional. You can trend out the conduct from 2003 to 2014 and see that between anti-kickback and misbranding, we see more enforcement activity in one bucket than the other. Perhaps we see more of a shift toward the anti-kickback these days because of some developments in the case law, including the *Caronia* case,[5] in which certain off-label marketing practices under specific facts were granted First Amendment protection— thereby making it more difficult for the government to argue that off-label promotion resulted in false claims. However, it is not something that you want to say with certainty because many False Claims Act cases are still under seal. It is more a matter of which issues are coming to their attention from relators, whether the government chooses to intervene, and then how they move forward as a result of the available evidence.

The most interesting pieces of these developments are how they get settled. Corporate integrity agreements (CIAs) exhibit some new trends with respect

---

[3] False Claims Act, 31 U.S.C. § 3729-3733 (2012).
[4] *Johnson & Johnson to Pay More Than $2.2 Billion to Resolve Criminal and Civil Investigations*, U.S. DEP'T. OF JUSTICE (Nov. 4, 2013), http://www.justice.gov/opa/pr/2013/November/13-ag-1170.html.
[5] *United States v. Caronia*, 703 F.3d 149 (2nd Cir. 2012).

to the type of compliance included. We are seeing that The Office of the Inspector General (OIG) and The Department of Health and Human Services (HHS) require more oversight and more direct involvement on the exercising of the compliance piece from the company's board of directors. Senior management officers are certifying compliance with CIAs, so there is more personal responsibility involved. All that is a way of trying to ensure that the culture and the compliance tone is appropriate at the organization. This is really an interpretation of the *Caremark*[6] case.

We are also seeing an increasing number of provisions included in CIAs that provide for compensation clawback in the contracts of senior executives. Other trends include ensuring that companies are not inappropriately incentivizing their sales forces to engage in inappropriate promotional activity. There have always been provisions in CIAs that require incentive compensation programs to comply with the law, but we have been seeing increasingly stronger provisions in recent CIAs.

Briefly, the civil False Claims Act[7] continues to be used extensively in health care fraud enforcement in large part due to how the actions are brought to the government by *qui tam* relators. The False Claims Act has been defined and interpreted very broadly through the years. This Act also was expanded in the Affordable Care Act in key ways that impact compliance programs—such as codifying the "one purpose" rule as the intent standard and the "boot strap" theory that a kickback can form the basis for a false claim.

With respect to the False Claims Act, it is important to remember that the submission, or the facilitation, of a claim is among the items that trigger liability if the claim is false—inaccurate, incomplete or untruthful. This means, for example, that an indirect biller such as a manufacturer that does not submit claims for payment to the government like a provider does, can submit a false claim through the facilitation aspect. Note that many states have state civil false claim statutes that are as stringent as the federal False Claims Act.[8] This is a direct result of prior legislation that incented states to enact such legislation to share in settlement dollars.

---

[6] *U.S., ex rel. Ramadoss v. Caremark Inc.*, 586 F. Supp. 2d 668 (W.D. Tex. 2008).
[7] 31 U.S.C. §§ 3729-33.
[8] *Id.*

Defending Clients

We want to argue the law and the facts of the case in light of the law. Is the conduct violative of the law? Is it unclear? What are the facts and circumstances of the conduct? What was the state of the law? It is critical to freeze in time the state of the law and when the alleged violations occurred.

Depending on the different time periods, you may be addressing different laws and sub regulatory guidance. The Civil False Claims Act has up to a ten-year statute of limitations.

It is one thing if you have a very narrow time period in connection with a product or a service offering, but many times government inquiries involve longer periods of time. During the time periods, there are inevitable changes in the laws. Now, more than ever, work with organizations to teach employees how to use email and other non-standard electronically stored information systems correctly. Document retention programs also must be implemented.

Relators

Qui tam relators, or whistleblowers, who present information alleging potential misconduct under the False Claims Act to the Department of Justice pursuant to the Civil False Claims Act continue to be the most common way health care fraud investigations are initiated. If information is presented to a prosecutor, there is a procedure described in the false claims statute as to how the case will proceed during the investigation. For example, the statute includes, by way of example only, certain time frames including how long the case may remain under seal by the court, before an intervention decision is made by the prosecutors as to whether they will decide to move forward with the case on behalf of the relator.

Who are relators? Many times a relator is a disgruntled employee who has previously reported the potential misconduct internally prior to reporting it to the Department of Justice. Generally, an employee will inform a direct report, supervisor or member in the compliance department of his/her concerns. It is only after the organization fails to act, or fails to act in a satisfactory manner, that the employee is aware that the report is made externally. Relators may feel disappointed that the concern has not been given attention, taken seriously, and/or addressed for one reason or another. The relator then believes that there is no other option than to report the potential misconduct outside the organization to the law enforcement authorities.

Relators often bring their evidence of alleged misconduct to the enforcement authority with counsel and present it to them to, among other things, effectuate change in the organization. It is significant to note that the Civil False Claims Act provides a significant share of any recovery, should there be a recovery, be shared with the relator. Interestingly, even if the government declines to intervene in the case and the relator pursues the case on his/her own without the assistance of the government, the government then shares in the relator's recovery. The statutory framework does incentive external reporting.

There have been some interesting law review articles and other publications written by professors and others who study relator trends inside and outside the health care and life sciences industries. Specifically, they examine the whistleblower personality. At the end of the day, it is critical for an organization to establish an effective corporate compliance program. This means that there must be a culture that genuinely promotes employees communicating with internal personnel and seeking comfort that concerns will be addressed without retaliation.

I go back to my previous observation that it is very difficult to hire a person to serve as a chief compliance officer. The person must, on top of all the academic credential and skill sets required, have the ability to maintain this culture and be a "people person." Organizations should establish open door policies that allow employees to voice concerns in a meaningful, non-threatening way, with no ramifications.

These concerns must then be acknowledged, addressed as appropriate, and wrong doers must be disciplined. No one wants to be ignored if they report a potential wrongdoing—communication is key with the individuals who express these concerns. We have seen with some regularity that disgruntled employees are going to do something about their grievances when they feel that no one within the organization is listening, and sometimes that means taking a matter outside the organization.

Worst Practices

With respect to manufacturers, issues that will continue to raise scrutiny include the following: inappropriate interactions with health care professionals, such as offering items in exchange for a referral or entering into contracts that are not bona fide contracts on appropriate commercial terms, and data purchase agreements that are purchased when the data is not really needed, or paying for services when the services are not really needed or no one ever does anything with the information obtained from the services. If the intent behind these payments is nothing but to induce a referral for the item or the service that is reimbursed by the federal health care program, it is going to be problematic. Also problematic is paying for things on behalf of the provider or health care professional that the institution should be paying for itself, such as equipment or subsidizing their capital expenditures.

Challenges for Clients

It is very difficult to defend cases brought under a civil false claims case as the defendant is not presented a complaint initially. Rather, a subpoena is issued to investigate factually whether a complaint will be filed in connection with the intervention decision. As such, a company is disadvantaged with the procedural process. It is unlike any other type of litigation. Initially, a company is solely guessing what the potential wrongdoing under investigation includes.

Cooperation is always the best course of action. There are many reasons why cooperation is important, but the number one challenge is the mandatory and permissive exclusion laws, both of which the OIG has jurisdiction over. To the extent that the company is found guilty of certain violations of laws, there may be mandatory exclusion from participation in the federal health care programs; other violations trigger permissive exclusion by the OIG, where the OIG may exercise discretion as to whether it will exercise its exclusion authority. Mandatory exclusion means a product or service is not going to be reimbursed by a federal health care program for a certain period of time. Time frames are set out in the regulations and may be very lengthy. Permissive exclusion may be waived at the discretion of the OIG in exchange for consideration—such consideration typically involves the company entering into a corporate integrity agreement with the OIG for a set period of time.

Corporate Integrity Agreements

As mentioned above, a CIA is entered into as consideration for the OIG not exercising its permissive exclusion authority. It is a contract between the company and the OIG that generally lasts five to seven years. Pursuant to the terms of the CIA, the company agrees to create, or to maintain, a currently existing, corporate compliance infrastructure. There is an annual independent review of the compliance program by a third party organization. The OIG assigns a "monitor" to interact with the company under the CIA and the third party organization that reviews the company compliance activities.

CIAs include provisions that address a compliance officer, a compliance committee, board oversight, certifications, training (usually for the entire organization), auditing, monitoring, and open door policies. The company must report to the government all "reportable events" which are defined in the CIA. Numerous reports are made throughout the CIA period and the OIG will make site visit(s). The OIG is interested in ensuring future regulatory compliance and preventing repeat offenders.

Top Compliance Issues

Compliance programs have evolved generally. There has been time for organizations to better understand what works better within their organization, for their personnel and within their corporate culture. There is no one size fits all. There are better practices and lessons learned, however. Compliance program elements for an effective compliance program are described generally in the United States Federal Sentencing Guidelines[9] for Organization. The OIG also has articulated these elements in health care industry specific voluntary compliance guidances over the year.

Compliance challenges continue to exist within each organization. It is to be expected. Some infrastructure questions permeate as to the separation of the legal and compliance functions. While the Health Exchange regulations require the separation of the legal and compliance function, most of the other OIG voluntary compliance guidances do not have such a requirement. Some CIAs require such separation from a contractual perspective.

---

[9] U.S. SENTENCING GUIDELINES MANUAL § 8A1.1-8F1.1 (2013).

With respect to the elements of compliance generally that are challenging, the conducting of effective training is always going to be one that many organizations find difficult. For example, a lot goes into a web-based training, but the question is, is that really effective? Are employees just clicking through and taking a test?

The concept of monitoring is one that companies are getting a little bit better at, but it is still a challenge. It is the same with auditing. It is very difficult to figure out exactly how to conduct audits and to get the resources to figure out how to audit and not creep into other areas. Technology is helping, but you cannot go to every speaker program and you cannot be with every sales representative. For these reasons, monitoring and auditing in certain pieces of the health care sector is very difficult.

The other piece of the challenge is convincing your employees that bringing compliance matters to the attention of someone in the organization will not result in retaliation. This whole concept of non-retaliation can be difficult for employees to believe. As much as you may publicize an anonymous hotline, folks are still afraid of retaliation.

Every organization is different as it relates to compliance; there is no one size that fits all with respect to the different challenges associated with regulatory compliance. Still, one of the most important pieces to a successful compliance program is finding the right chief compliance officer. This person not only has the right background by means of training, education, experience, and expertise to fill that role but, on top of everything else, is the friendly face to all the employees—someone they can trust, someone they believe, someone in touch with the culture of the company, someone who is not just at the top of an organizational chart. This is someone who has to instill trust at all levels of an organization. That is a difficult role to fill. That job position is so challenging that I often get involved with helping organizations interview and select the right people for the role.

There is a lot of debate and there are a lot of questions out there with respect to hiring someone for a chief compliance role. Do you want someone who has legal training and a legal background, or someone more on the financial side to get the auditing, monitoring, and technology piece? That decision is really left to the organizations. I believe that the legal background is the best background, but I have also seen successful chief compliance officers who have come from a financial background. It really depends on the person. If they come from a financial background, they need legal support to understand the policies and procedures and have questions on how to do the internal investigations, how to interact with people in legal, or how to interact with outside counsel that they hire. I have also seen very successful chief compliance officers from other backgrounds. Again, the primary concern is that the chief compliance officer be an effective resource to the organization when it comes to fostering an open door compliance environment.

The Stark Law

There is strict liability with respect to the Stark Law[10] and we have some developments under way with respect to the enforcement side. The Stark Law is a prohibition against physician self-referrals for designated health services. The intent is to prevent conflicts of interests—to ban physicians from referring to designed health services in which they have an ownership or equity interest or financial relationship (e.g., employment agreement) unless an exception applies. As we have this new round of integration because of the Affordable Care Act, there is much Stark analysis to be done. This is because of the integration between the doctors and the hospitals including shared risk arrangements, Accountable Care Organizations (ACOs), and other arrangements.

Conclusion

Organizations in the health care and life sciences industries—both veterans and emerging companies—face an ever-evolving set of compliance-oriented challenges. It becomes increasingly important for organizations to adopt effective corporate compliance programs and foster an inclusive atmosphere of compliance. That being said, it also falls upon attorneys to stay up to date on the laws and regulatory guidance so that they may assist clients in navigating these challenges. As I mentioned before, we forever play the role of the student—we are constantly faced with new regulations and enforcement trends so that we may best advise our clients accordingly.

---

[10] 42 U.S.C. § 1395nn.

Looking Ahead

We are going to continue to see changes in how states work through Health Exchange implementation and Health Reform generally. We also are going to continue to address regulatory changes with respect to different pieces of Affordable Care Act implementation. It is going to take some time to get this information. There is not yet even a full year of data that needs to be collected and analyzed to understand what the impact is as it relates to access, quality, and cost. Did it shift the population that now has insurance? Are the penalties for noncompliance being enforced? There is much that remains to be seen. The interesting thing about the Affordable Care Act is the litigation just keeps coming with respect to different pieces of it and that will certainly continue.

There are certain pieces where, as we spend time thinking about them and implementing them, clients have decisions to make with respect to taking this to the next level from a litigation perspective. There are many decision points for organizations to make in terms of what to do next. Some of it is strategic, based on what competitors are doing.

These decisions are being talked about and decided at a very high level. We talk about the ramifications and then work with the statute and the regulations. We take advantage of comment periods and meeting with folks in Washington. That is the process and that is the counseling. We are working to interpret pieces of it and figure pieces out as we go.

Advice for Attorneys

Do an assessment of compliance in the organization—a gap assessment is critical. Working with senior management and the board of directors to try to get past the concept of compliance as a cost center sets the tone and the culture of the organization. Compliance should really become the DNA of the organization so that people know to do the right thing regardless of what piece of the health care or life sciences delivery system they are in. There is not one strategy that is going to get an organization there, and it is not one person who can do it; this is going to take the village. It is like SOX compliance, although it is a little bit more difficult to convince people sometimes because it is not just a financial control, but a business control.

Key Takeaways

- It is important to understand that the law is having trouble keeping up with technology. Attorneys must spend time with their clients going through what the current law says with respect to compliance regulations and help them determine the best course of action for their organization. It is difficult to refer to case law because there is not much of it out there right now.

- In defending clients, be sure to look at what the law said at the time of the allegations of noncompliance. The law is constantly changing, so it is critical to look back and see if laws were different at the time of the alleged violation.

- You must take your time investigating the claim, and you may have to interview people who are no longer working at the organization. It is crucial to establish what a person's intent was with their noncompliance, which may take a long time. But in the end it is worth it to know all of the details.

- Finding the right chief compliance officer for an organization is something an attorney may have to help their clients do. It should be someone who employees can trust and who also has the right combination of education, training, and experience.

- It is critical to work with senior management and the board to make them understand that compliance is more than just a cost center. It is actually very important to the long-term success of their organization.

Wendy C. Goldstein is a member of the Cooley LLP's business department and is a partner in the firm's Health Care and Life Sciences Regulatory practice. She is a resident in the New York office. Ms. Goldstein concentrates in health care fraud and abuse and government health care program matters relevant to manufacturers, suppliers, providers, payors, and other ancillary providers in the health care and life sciences spaces. She also represents those entities that invest in such concerns.

Specifically, Ms. Goldstein is involved with: (1) Counseling clients regarding the research, manufacture, sale, promotion, distribution, pricing, and import/export of pharmaceuticals, biologics, and medical devices including such topics as fraud and abuse, the Food, Drug, and Cosmetic Act (FDCA), the Prescription Drug Marketing Act

(PDMA), third party coverage and reimbursement (government and commercial), Medicaid Drug Rebate and other government pricing programs, corporate compliance, privacy, antitrust, Medicare Part D program, transparency laws and other state law issues; (2) Counseling regarding government health care program compliance risks, including designing, implementing, and assessing the effectiveness of corporate compliance programs; conducting board of directors training; conducting internal investigations relating to compliance matters; providing self-disclosure counsel; preparing Office of the Inspector General of Department of Health and Human Services (OIG) advisory opinion requests; drafting and negotiating co-promote agreements, drug rebate agreements, supply chain arrangements, fee-for-service agreements, and third party vendor agreements; conducting health regulatory due diligences; (3) defending pharmaceutical manufacturers in all phases of government investigations and inquiries, and negotiating settlement agreements and OIG corporate integrity agreements on behalf of manufacturers in connection with the resolution of qui tam and other government actions; (4) counseling third party payors in connection with the delivery of outpatient prescription drug benefit and specialty drug benefit programs offered under insured (commercial and government) and self-insured products.

Prior to joining Cooley, Ms. Goldstein served as a partner in the New York office of a leading law firm specializing in, among other practices, health care and life sciences where she was the chair of the firm's Health Care and Life Sciences Practice Steering Committee and the Pharmaceutical Industry Health Regulatory Practice Group. Ms. Goldstein speaks and writes extensively on issues relating to fraud and abuse, board governance, government program pricing, corporate compliance, government enforcement activity relevant to the life sciences and managed care industries, and health care reform. She is a contributing author to the ABA Health Law Section Pharmaceutical Law treatise. Ms. Goldstein has served as an adjunct professor of health care fraud and abuse at Pace University School of Law. She also has served on several advisory boards for industry publications and legal associations including the New York State Bar Association Committee on Medical Research and Biotechnology and the New York City Bar Committee on Bioethical Issues. Ms. Goldstein serves on the board of directors of several nonprofit health care associations and educational institutions. She also is actively involved in pro bono activities relating to the pediatric oncology research and other health care education and access initiatives. Ms. Goldstein has been ranked by Chambers USA as one of America's leading lawyers for health care (2008 to 2014). She was selected for inclusion in The Best Lawyers in America *(2013 and 2014) and in* New York Super Lawyers—Metro *(2006 to 2014), which cited her among its "Top 100" (2010 to 2014) and its "Top 50 Women" (2006, 2007, and 2009 to 2014). Ms. Goldstein was also selected as a Life Science Star in LMG Life Sciences 2012 and*

2013 and was named by LMG as "Attorney of the Year" for Health Care Pricing and Reimbursement in 2013. She was recognized as a leading lawyer in the 2012 Legal 500 United States in the Health Care Insurer category. She was named as one of Nightingale's Outstanding Young Health Care Lawyers in 2007.

Acknowledgment: I am grateful to my colleagues at Cooley LLP, especially those in the Health Care and Life Sciences Regulatory practice group. We know that no woman is an island. In a regulatory practice where the legal landscape is evolving at a rapid pace, and in an industry that innovates even faster than the law, it is all about the talent and support of our colleagues.

I would also like to thank Ms. Lauren Prial for her editorial assistance with this chapter.

Dedication: To my wonderful parents, I am forever grateful.

Helping Clients Comply
with the Affordable Care Act

Laura Miller Andrew

Partner and Health Care Practice Leader

Smith Gambrell & Russell LLP

ASPATORE

Introduction

As an employee benefits and health care attorney, I have been working with employers for many years on the design and implementation of their employee benefit plans. Specifically, I have concentrated my practice on what are commonly known as "welfare benefits" (e.g., health care, life insurance, disability coverage, etc.). In this role, I have worked with many large and small employers on the provision of health care to their employees through employer-sponsored health insurance coverage. This chapter is focused on how employers can navigate through the provisions of the Affordable Care Act (ACA),[1] including the "Play or Pay" employer mandate, and other related laws in providing employer-sponsored health insurance coverage to their employees. Be warned, this chapter is focused on strategies and general advice and is not intended to be a "play by play" implementation guide for employers on the ACA.

The Affordable Care Act: Legislating Through Regulations and Guidance

Contrary to the standard process for such important legislation, which usually involves bipartisan support and hours of debate and consideration before final passage, the ACA was largely passed by Democrats without the support of Republicans, and with little or no debate on the provisions of the Bill. Therefore, the ACA is a "barebones" law without the "meat" provided by the discussions and conferences that such laws generally have. In the absence of such guidance from the Congressional Record, the implementing agencies, such as the Internal Revenue Service (IRS) and the United States Department of Labor (DOL) have essentially been legislating through regulations and guidance. Provisions that seem to have one meaning based on the plain text of the law are being interpreted to mean something else entirely when the implementing agencies' regulations and guidance are released. Consequently, practitioners should tread carefully when advising their clients because the meaning of the ACA can shift at any time with the release of each new regulation, notice, or guidance. This ambiguity has also resulted in a large number of lawsuits about various aspects of the ACA. For example, multiple lawsuits have been filed about the provision of subsidies to individual taxpayers. The ACA states that qualifying individuals can get a subsidy for health

---

[1] Patient Protection and Affordable Care Act, Pub. L. No. 111-148, 124 Stat. 119 (2010).

insurance coverage that they purchase through a state health care exchange or marketplace. The ACA does not, however, mention the ability to receive a subsidy on the federal default health care exchanges—but the IRS is allowing individuals to claim subsidies on these exchanges.

Ultimately, the "meat" on the "bones" of the ACA will be developed through regulations, notices, guidance, and court cases that evolve out of the enforcement of the ACA. In the meantime, employers need to prepare for full implementation of the ACA, including the employer mandate (i.e., "Play of Pay"), by using their best judgment to comply with its provisions, and relying on the advice of legal counsel and other advisors to assist them in navigating through the ACA and its requirements.

Impacts of the Affordable Care Act on Employers and Individuals

Since the ACA[2] was signed into law on March 23, 2010, the provision of health insurance coverage to individuals in the United States has been fundamentally altered. Prior to the passage of the ACA, individuals were not required to have health insurance, and employers were not required to provide it. Even if employers offered health insurance, they were not required to have any particular kind of health insurance plan. Generally, they could design their health insurance plan based on their needs and the needs of their employees, as long as the plan complied with applicable law. Such laws include the provisions of the Health Insurance Portability and Accountability Act (HIPAA),[3] which requires portability of health care coverage and protection of sensitive medical information related to employer-provided health insurance coverage, and the Consolidated Omnibus Budget Reconciliation Act of 1985 (COBRA),[4] which requires continuation of coverage rights. Although employers had wide latitude in the specifics of the group health insurance plans that they offered, such as co-pays and deductibles, such plans also were required to provide benefit parity with respect to aggregate lifetime and annual dollar limits for mental health benefits by the Mental Health Parity Act of 1996 (MHPA).[5]

---

[2] *Id.*

[3] Health Insurance Portability and Accountability Act of 1996, Pub. L. No. 104-191, 110 Stat. 1936.

[4] Consolidated Omnibus Budget Reconciliation Act of 1985, Pub. L. No. 99-272, 100 Stat. 82.

[5] Mental Health Parity Act of 1996, Pub. L. No. 104-204, 110 Stat. 2945.

Additional requirements were added by the Mental Health Parity and Addiction Equity Act of 2008 (MHPAEA)[6] to ensure that financial requirements (such as co-pays, deductibles, etc.) and treatment limitations (such as visit limits) applicable to mental health or substance use disorder (MH/SUD) benefits are no more restrictive than the predominant requirements or limitations applied to substantially all medical/surgical benefits. Otherwise, an employer was free to design a health insurance plan that provided only basic medical services or provided broad-based coverage for all medical conditions.

Generally, employers offered coverage either through (1) a self-insured group health plan (sometimes called a "self-funded" plan) where the employer pays out-of-pocket for all health insurance claims as they are incurred; or (2) a fully-insured group health insurance plan where the employer pays a fixed premium to an insurance carrier for the coverage. Subject to certain nondiscrimination restrictions for self-insured plans that were implemented to ensure that employers offer the same or similar coverage to the average non-highly compensated employee as they offer to executives and other highly-compensated employees, employers were free to decide which employees to cover and how many hours their employees needed to work to be eligible for health insurance coverage. Now, under the ACA, these nondiscrimination requirements have been extended to fully-insured plans. (Please note that, as regulations and guidance have not yet been issued in this area, employers do not yet have to comply with these new rules for fully-insured plans, but, guidance is expected in the not-too-distant future.) Additionally, employers can no longer choose how many hours an employee must work to be eligible for health insurance benefits. If an employer decides to offer health insurance coverage to its employees, then under the ACA, it must offer coverage to all "full-time" employees. The ACA defines "full-time" to mean working 30 hours or more in a workweek, which many employers would not usually consider to be "full-time" for other purposes.

Another key aspect of the ACA is its so-called "employer mandate," commonly referred to as the employer "Play or Pay" requirement, (which has been postponed until 2015). The employer mandate requires employers

---

[6] Mental Health Parity and Addiction Equity Act of 2008, Pub. L. No. 110-343, 122 Stat. 3881.

to offer a specific level of health insurance coverage to their full-time employees or pay an excise tax penalty to the federal government. There are three ways that can result in an employer being required to pay a penalty:

1. The employer can decide to offer *no* health insurance coverage;
2. The employer can offer health insurance coverage that does not meet the ACA standards; or
3. The employer can offer health insurance coverage that meets the standards, but is not "affordable."

Specifically, as of January 1, 2015, employers with more than a specified number of full-time equivalent employees must offer "qualified health insurance coverage" to 95 percent (70 percent for 2015 only) of their "full-time" employees and the coverage must be "affordable." If an employer does not offer this "qualified health insurance coverage" (sometimes called "minimum essential coverage") to its employees and at least one of its employees enrolls in a health care exchange and receives a subsidy, then the employer must pay an excise tax penalty. Employers who employ an average of at least 50 (100 in 2015) "full-time employees" during the preceding calendar year must comply ("applicable large employers"). For this calculation, an employer must include its full-time employees and any "full-time equivalents," (combining the monthly hours of all employees who work part-time and dividing that number by 120). Effective as of January 1, 2015, if an applicable large employer offers no coverage (i.e., it does not provide "minimum essential coverage") to 95 percent (70 percent in 2015) of its full-time employees and at least one employee receives a subsidy for coverage through a health care exchange, then the employer will be subject to a $2,000 annual excise tax penalty for each full-time employee (calculated monthly), including those that did not go to a health care exchange. This excise tax penalty is calculated based on the number of full-time employees after subtracting the first 30 (in 2015 substitute "80" for "30" to reduce the penalty).

This excise tax penalty can be quite expensive. For example, if an applicable large employer offers no health insurance coverage and has 100 full-time employees, 20 of whom receive a subsidy for the year in a health care exchange, then the employer will owe $2,000 for each full-time employee (minus 30), for a "Play or Pay" excise tax penalty of $140,000 ($2,000 x 70 employees (i.e., 100-30)). In 2015, this excise tax penalty will be slightly reduced, as the employer will owe $2,000 for each full-time employee (minus 80) for a penalty amount of $40,000 ($2,000 x 20 employees (i.e., 100-80)). This "Play or Pay" penalty is an excise tax and is *not* a deductible business expense for the employer, whereas contributions an employer makes for health insurance coverage are usually deductible business expenses.

If an employer decides to avoid the excise tax penalty by "Playing," that is, providing health insurance coverage as required by the ACA, then it must now offer specific types of coverage to certain qualifying individuals with specific cost structures. This coverage, called "qualified health insurance coverage" under the ACA is coverage that:

1. Provides the essential health benefits package prescribed by the ACA;
2. Limits annual cost-sharing and co-pays;
3. Does not require cost-sharing for preventive services or immunizations; and
4. Provides coverage to certain dependent children.

This means that employers no longer have the flexibility to design their health insurance plans based on their own needs and desires and are now limited in how they can control the cost of health insurance through plan design. Health insurance coverage must now be "affordable" as defined by the ACA. If the portion of the health insurance premium that an employee is required to pay for employee-only coverage exceeds 9.5 percent of such employee's household income, then the coverage is considered "unaffordable" and the employer will be subject to an excise tax penalty if such employee receives coverage through a health care exchange and receives a subsidy. Therefore, if an applicable large employer offers insufficient coverage (i.e., the coverage does not provide "minimum value" (MV) or is "unaffordable"), and if at least one full-time employee obtains a subsidy through a health care exchange, then the employer will be required to pay the lesser of (1) $3,000 for each full-time employee receiving a subsidy; or (2) $2,000 for each full-time employee (after subtracting the first 30 full-time employees). As explained above, in 2015 only, subtract the first 80 full-time employees. For example, if an employer offers qualified health insurance coverage and has 100 full-time employees, 20 of whom receive a subsidy for the year, because the coverage was "unaffordable" when enrolling in a health care exchange, then the employer will owe $3,000 for each employee receiving a subsidy; thus, owing a "Play or Pay" excise tax penalty of $60,000. Please note that the excise tax penalty is capped at the amount of the excise tax penalty that would have been assessed for a failure to provide any health insurance coverage, or $140,000 ($2,000 x 70 employees (i.e., 100-30 or 100-80 for 2015)). Therefore, an employer would be subject to the calculated excise tax penalty of $60,000, as it is less than the maximum amount of $140,000.

Employees do not have a choice either. Generally, subject to certain limited exceptions, under the ACA, all individuals in the United States must have health insurance coverage or pay a penalty. The penalty will gradually increase over the next 3 years. As of January 1, 2014, the penalty is the greater of $95 or 1 percent of household income in excess of the tax filing threshold. By 2016, the penalty will be the greater of $695 or 2.5 percent of income in excess of the tax filing threshold. Individuals can receive their coverage through an individual insurance policy or otherwise, or through employer-provided coverage.

Demonstrating compliance with "Play or Pay" requirements for both employers and employees will require substantial documentation. Under Sections 6055 and 6056 of the ACA,[7] employers must collect and provide certain information to the IRS so that it can figure out whether they are meeting the mandated health insurance coverage obligations and whether each individual employee is meeting his or her mandated health insurance requirements. Insurance companies and self-insured health plans are required to provide a variety of information about each insured individual's health insurance coverage, such as (1) each insured individual's health insurance coverage; (2) how many people are covered; and (3) what they pay toward the cost of the coverage. In addition, every employer that is subject to the employer mandate has to complete paperwork describing a large number of data collection points. All of this information has to be distributed to individuals as shown on the attached Appendix B, which is entitled Affordable Care Act Information Reporting Requirements. To add to the complexity of the situation, the tax forms that must be completed have not yet been released by the IRS. Simply put, not only do employers need to provide health insurance coverage and

---

[7] Patient Protection and Affordable Care Act §§ 6055, 6056.

keep track of who has what coverage, they now have to ensure that they have and maintain accurate information, so that they can correctly complete and submit these new tax forms.

Next year, applicable large employers need to be ready to start collecting the information for their 2015 returns without the benefit of review of the new tax forms. As a result, a large administrative burden is currently being placed on employers—not only do they have to offer health insurance coverage, they must also document what kind of health insurance coverage they are offering, and they have to figure out whether they will "Play or Pay." Consequently, many employers are hiring consultants, attorneys, and actuaries—who have now become a central part of compliance with the ACA. Providing health insurance coverage to employees is no longer an optional fringe benefit for employers. It is now a requirement unless an employer wants to "Pay" under the employer "Play or Pay" mandate.

Compliance with Health Insurance Reform Laws, Regulations, and Guidance

There are several layers involved in health insurance reform compliance. The first layer, as noted above, involves the new IRS tax forms associated with Sections 6055 and 6056, which must be given to both the IRS and all individuals who participate in an employer's group health plan. In addition, employers have to determine whether they may be facing any excise tax penalties under the "Play or Pay" provisions. If so, they must document and pay the excise tax penalties to the IRS. To determine the total amount of any excise tax penalty, employers must also figure out which of their employees are subject to the mandated coverage requirement. As mentioned above, all full-time employees who work for 30 or more hours per week must be offered health insurance coverage. While Bills have been introduced in both the House and the Senate that would change the full-time status requirement to 40 hours per week, it is unlikely that any of these Bills will be passed in the near future.

In February 2014, the IRS released final regulations on the safe harbor methods that employers can use to determine which of their employees are "full time." Unfortunately, the methodology for this calculation is complex. It involves using a new concept of "measurement periods." While the safe harbor methods distinguish between new employees and ongoing employees, hours are counted for both groups during these "measurement periods," which must be at least 3—and no more than 12—consecutive months long. For new employees, this period is referred to as an "initial measurement period." For ongoing employees, this period is referred to as a "standard measurement period." Following this initial or standard measurement period, is the "stability period." The stability period is the "hold period" during which those employees are locked into full-time or part-time status based on the number of hours that they worked during the initial measurement period or standard measurement period, regardless of how many hours that they work during the stability period. Generally, the stability period must be at least 6 consecutive calendar months and no shorter than the initial or standard measurement period. For example, if the employer chose a 7-month standard measurement period for that type of employee, then the stability period would also have to be at least 7 months.) Employers have one more measurement period that they can utilize in this determination—an "administrative period." This optional administrative period can be utilized by an employer to complete its determination of which employees are full-time under the ACA definition, and provides time to then notify and enroll any eligible employees in health insurance coverage. This administrative period cannot exceed 90 days.

To add to the complexity, different measurement periods can be used for different employee classifications—i.e., salary vs. hourly, or headquarters vs. field. Additionally, once an employee has completed an initial measurement period, that employee must be switched to the standard measurement period that is used for all employees in his or her classification. This determination is not straightforward, it can be very difficult in operation, especially when you consider the many different types of employees: temporary employees, seasonal employees, and variable-hour employees. Educational institutions, airlines, hospitals, and certain other specific work forces also have special rules to determine the status of their employees. Employers may also have employees that do not fit neatly into a specific classification, such as employees who are not exactly seasonal, but who only work for certain periods of time. For example, some construction workers might work for an employer for 6 months on one project and leave after the project is completed—only to return 2 months later when there is another project on which they want to work. Counting these employees' measurement periods can be very complex.

Unfortunately, in some cases, even if an employer uses its best judgment to provide health insurance coverage to eligible employees and their eligible dependents and completes and files all of the new IRS forms, 3 or 4 years down the road, the IRS may still audit the employer and determine that the forms were not correctly completed and not all eligible individuals received coverage as required by the ACA. At that time, the IRS can assess back excise tax penalties (including interest) for not complying with the "Play or Pay" mandate. Therefore, I suggest to my clients is that they develop a methodology for the measurement periods for *every* single class of employee and job title. Basically, employers need to determine what period of time they are going to use for each measurement period and document, in writing, why they chose such period. This written documentation should be retained in their plan records. These internal records can then be used as proof that they attempted, in good faith, to comply with the requirements promulgated by the multiple agencies that are interpreting and enforcing the ACA. In addition, I recommend that employers retain legal counsel early for assistance with the process. If issues arise later with any of the various implementing agencies that are in charge of enforcing the ACA, the prior utilization of legal counsel to review and analyze full-time employee status will be an additional factor showing good faith compliance. According to comments from the various agencies, at this time, good faith compliance may be sufficient to avoid and/or mitigate any potential penalties and interest that could arise during a later audit. Essentially, the best way for an employer to protect itself is to: (1) follow the ACA regulations, notices, and other guidance as closely as possible; (2) engage competent counsel; and (3) document such good faith compliance efforts and measures.

There is also a tool on the DOL website that employers can utilize to conduct an ACA self-audit. This assists employers in documenting their good faith compliance efforts and measures. As the DOL has a 6-year statute of limitations and the IRS has a 3-year statute of limitations, it is wise for employers to utilize this tool and document their good faith efforts to comply with all provisions of the ACA.[8] In addition, it is unclear, at this time, when the statute of limitations will begin to run. For example, with regard to Form 5500s, if they are not fully completed, the IRS and DOL can take the position that the statute of limitations never began. If an

---

[8] *See Self Compliance Tool for Part 7 of ERISA: Affordable Care Act Provisions*, U.S. DEP'T OF LABOR, *available at* http://www.dol.gov/ebsa/pdf/part7-2.pdf.

employer is audited by an agency in the future with regard to ACA compliance, then it will be able to show documented good faith compliance if it maintains detailed records of its own internal controls and self-audits—even in a situation where the necessary forms to comply with the ACA have not yet been released (e.g., the new required 6055 and 6056 forms).

Enforcement of the ACA and Audit Triggers

At the present time, for 2014, employers do not need to meet the "minimum value" requirements of the employer "Play or Pay" requirements. The only real requirement is that if they offer a group health plan, it must generally comply with the essential health benefit requirements described above and required under ACA. Cost factors are generally not yet relevant because the "Play or Pay" mandate has been extended until 2015. It should be noted that there are still a few "grandfathered" plans in existence that have met the stringent rules in the ACA to remain "frozen" so that they do not need to meet many of the ACA essential health benefit requirements, such as 100 percent coverage of preventive care without co-pays. However, plan sponsors still need to ensure that any such plans comply with the "grandfather" rules and send the appropriate notices about their grandfathered status.

An important new enforcement agency with respect to the ACA is the Occupational Safety and Health Administration (OSHA). Under OSHA regulations, if an employer retaliates against an employee after he or she reports such employer for not providing the health benefits required by the ACA, such as offering dependent child coverage up to age 26, then he or she can bring a whistleblower claim against such employer—and if the employee does, that claim will be overseen by OSHA. This type of claim can also be a trigger for enforcement investigations.

As previously noted, while the ACA is enforced by many governmental agencies, it is enforced most commonly by the IRS and DOL. The number of IRS and DOL audits in this area has increased exponentially in recent years and both the IRS and DOL have expanded the type of information that they are requesting during audits. One area that the IRS seems to be particularly concentrating on is whether employers are properly classifying individuals who are performing services for them as employees rather than independent contractors. In addition, the IRS is reconciling employer's Form 1099s for their independent contractors with the individuals' IRS filings. Some audits result from employers' failure to properly complete certain annual reporting requirements for their plans (e.g., Form 5500, etc.).

An ACA investigation may also be triggered in a situation where an employee has been fired, files a lawsuit, and adds an ACA issue as one of his or her claims. Alternatively, if an employee is not receiving health care coverage, and he or she believes that coverage should have been provided, a claim may be filed. Section 510 of the Employee Retirement Income Security Act (ERISA)[9] contains an anti-discrimination rule, which makes it unlawful to discharge, fine, suspend, expel, discipline, or discriminate against a participant or beneficiary for exercising any right to which such employee is entitled under the provisions of the plan or by law. Employers who are considering removing currently enrolled employees to reduce their headcount, should ensure that they do not violate ERISA Section 510. For example, if an employer reclassifies an employee to independent contractor status because it is reducing its headcount of full-time employees to avoid being subject to the "Play or Pay" mandate, it may trigger an ERISA Section 510 claim from one of such reclassified employee, and if such individual complains to the employer and is fired, a whistleblower claim under OSHA may also be filed.

Helping Clients Avoid ACA Audits

It is hard to advise clients whether they are likely to be the subject of an ACA audit—the IRS or DOL certainly will not tell you. In some cases, they will decide to audit a particular industry, such as restaurants or retail employers—and, occasionally, based on a complaint filed by an individual or a group of individuals. The IRS and DOL generally will not officially discuss their methodology for targeting certain employers. The best course of action for an employer is to ensure that any document or filing requested or required by the IRS or DOL is completed in a timely manner. If the IRS or DOL asks an employer to supply certain information, the employer should supply that information as soon as possible after checking with legal counsel, especially if the employer is unsure about what is being requested—to ensure that the information is presented properly and in a way that facilitates understanding of the facts by the IRS or DOL. Simply put, employers need to utilize best practices.

---

[9] Employee Retirement Income Security Act of 1974, Pub. L. No. 93-406, § 510, 88 Stat. 829.

Employers should keep all of their official health plan documents in one place. The best defense to an audit is to keep proper records, and to have the documentation available for inspection, and prepared in an orderly and organized fashion if requested by an IRS or DOL auditor. The most challenging aspect of the auditing process is the time and effort that is involved in assembling the documentation for the IRS or DOL. The IRS or DOL may ask for documents up front through a written request, such as Form W-2s, Form 1099s, and other payroll records. Normally, investigators give an employer the time to assemble the materials requested, and they are usually onsite for only a few days, unless the employer is very large or the audit is very complex. The IRS and DOL will often follow up with additional requests for documents before they complete the audit and deliver their audit findings. This is an area in which legal counsel can play a central role. Often, if legal counsel uncovers errors made by the employer during the process of assembling and reviewing the information requested by the IRS or DOL, legal counsel may be able to negotiate with the IRS or DOL to allow the employer to correct the errors during the audit process and avoiding any negative audit findings by the agent.

Top ACA Compliance Issues Impacting Health Care Clients

Complying with the ACA requirements in terms of co-pays, deductibles, and other components of health care law is very important. For example, a specific issue often comes up involving certain prescription drugs. In defining "essential health benefits," can an employer define it to only include generic drugs? Or, does the employer need to include brand-name drugs when no generic drug is available? As there is now a limit on the out-of-pocket expenses that a participant is required to pay under an ACA compliant plan, participants may not have an incentive to use a lower-cost generic drug when the participant hits the out-of-pocket maximums, since the participant will not have to pay the higher co-pay for the brand name drug. Based on some recently-released guidance, some employers are now defining only generic drugs (when medically necessary and appropriate) as essential health benefits, and considering brand-name drugs with higher-cost sharing as separate options that are not essential health benefits.

As discussed earlier in this chapter, the major issue for most employers is the "Play or Pay" analysis. As a reminder, if the employer is considered a large employer (generally, an employer with 50 or more full-time employees) and one or more of its employees receives a subsidy to help purchase health insurance coverage from a health care exchange, then the employer will pay an excise tax penalty (for 2015 only, employers with only 50 to 99 full-time equivalents generally are not subject to this penalty). An employee is eligible for a subsidy if his or her (1) household income is more than 133 percent or less than 400 percent of the federal poverty level; and (2) the employer's portion of the insurance premium on the employer's plan exceeds 9.5 percent of such employee's household income (that is, the coverage is "unaffordable").

An employee may only receive a subsidy if either (1) the employer offers no health insurance coverage to an employee, or (2) the coverage provided by the employer is not "qualified health coverage" that provides "minimum value," as discussed earlier in this chapter, or is unaffordable because the employee's premium exceeds 9.5 percent of such employee's household income. A qualified health plan provides minimum value if the percentage of allowed costs expected to be paid by the plan (not by the employees), in the aggregate, is at least 60 percent of such costs. United States Health and Human Services (HHS) has confirmed that the minimum value determination is made on an aggregate basis tested against national utilization data and is not on a plan-specific basis. HHS has provided a MV calculator.[10]

Employers must be careful to ensure that they do not unintentionally violate either prong of the test listed above. Regardless of whether an employer's plan is self-insured or fully-insured, it is important to ensure that it provides the minimum value coverage that is required, which may involve hiring an actuary. The employer must also ensure that it does not inadvertently violate the "affordability rule" mentioned above. Failure to comply with either prong may subject the employer to the "Play or Pay" excise tax penalties. As a reminder, these penalties are considered "excise taxes" and are not deductible business expenses.

There are also fees that must be paid by certain employers. The Transitional Reinsurance Program (TRP) is a program established by the ACA to stabilize health insurance premiums after the individual mandate became effective in 2014. The TRP collects payments from self-insured plans and

---

[10] *The Center for Consumer Information & Insurance Oversight*, CMS.GOV, http://cciio. cms.gov/resources/regulations/index.htmls.

health insurance issuers to offset a portion of high-cost medical claims that are expected to arise in the individual market during the first 3 years of the operation of the individual mandate. By no later than November 15 of 2014, 2015, and 2016, each contributing entity is required to submit an annual enrollment count of the number of covered lives subject to the TRP contribution to HHS. Within 30 days of submission of the annual enrollment count (or December 15, if later), HHS will notify the contributing entity of the total contribution it is required to pay. The assessment is expected to be due 30 days after receipt for the first TRP payment (approximately, January 15, 2015). The DOL has advised that TRP contributions may be paid from plan assets. If the TRP is paid by the plan sponsor, the IRS has said that the contributions would be deductible as ordinary and necessary business expenses under Code section 162.

Another fee that must be paid by self-insured health plans is the Patient-Centered Outcomes Research Institute (PCORI) Fees. PCORI's mission is to help people make informed health care decisions and improve health care delivery and outcomes by producing and promoting high-integrity, evidence-based information that comes from research guided by patients, caregivers, and the broader health care community. Self-insured group health plans must currently report and pay PCORI fees by July 31 of each year.

Best Practices for Complying with the ACA and Other Health Care Laws

To help our clients stay in compliance in this area, we try to ensure that we consult all guidance that has been issued from the IRS, the DOL, and other applicable agencies. We also attend many IRS and DOL conferences to find out as much as possible about any new or potential developments in this area so that we can guide our clients in complying with the rules. We communicate this information to our clients to ensure that they have as much information as possible to assist them with this difficult task.

In trying to stay on top of the requirements of the ACA, and handling all of the compliance tasks listed above, employers must also not forget about the other laws that impact group health plans. Specifically, employers with self-insured group health plans must also be aware of the laws and regulations promulgated under the HIPAA. For example, they should ensure that they have developed and implemented all required procedures, and prepared and distributed all appropriate notices required under HIPAA. At the same time, they must be aware of the general ERISA requirements (e.g., maintaining updated summary plan descriptions, summary of benefits and coverage, and other required plan documents and notices, etc.). They must also ensure that they are preparing required annual reports, such as the Form 5500. All of these requirements must be met in addition to the ACA requirements, which add to an already a complicated regulatory compliance structure.

The MHPA and the MHPAE and their specific requirements contain other important provisions. As mentioned briefly earlier in this chapter, if the group health plan meets the requirements of the ACA, but fails to meet the requirements of these two Acts, the plan may still be cited by the DOL or other governmental agencies for noncompliance. Specifically, if the group health plan fails to meet the requirements that mental health benefits be provided in a nondiscriminatory manner, both the DOL and participants may sue the plan for noncompliance.

Another common issue is failing to consider all plans that an employer provides to its employees. For example, some employers provide employees with a reimbursement account that they can use to pay certain health care expenses. These types of accounts are often called health reimbursement arrangements (HRAs). Under the ACA, beginning in 2014, HRAs must be integrated into an employer's group health plan or they will be considered to be separate group health plans that do not meet the requirements of the ACA. Failure to comply with the ACA provisions will result in excise taxes of $100 per person per day for each failure not corrected within 30 days. Therefore, in this example, if the HRA account is provided to 100 employees, the penalty could be $10,000 per day if the failure is not corrected within 30 days.

Unfortunately, employers also face a hefty penalty if they do not comply with the "Play or Pay" requirements of the ACA and other applicable laws (e.g., a $3,000 yearly penalty for each full-time employee that should have been covered but was not). If an employee receives a subsidy under a federal or state exchange, the employer may have to pay up to $2,000 per year for such employee. Even though the "Play or Pay" mandate for smaller employers has been postponed until 2016, it is certainly more challenging for smaller organizations to comply with these laws than larger organizations—primarily because they may not have an employee dedicated to maintenance of benefit plans and they may be depending on their insurance broker to help them. In such cases, brokers without sufficient expertise and knowledge could cause their clients to be assessed large penalties. Certainly, the penalties in this area could put a smaller company out of business.

Enhancing Existing Compliance Programs; Additional Issues

To help employers enhance existing compliance programs, legal counsel for employers should always start with the basics (i.e., make sure that their clients are complying with ERISA). For example, they should obtain all of their client's plan documents, summary plan descriptions, summary of benefits coverage, and HIPAA documents if the employer is self-insured. After fixing any mistakes in those areas, legal counsel should turn its attention to ACA compliance issues, which includes determining who is a full-time employee. Of course, at that time, look at the employer's health plan and any related documents to make sure that they comply with all applicable laws. We also recommend that legal counsel discuss with the employer the methodology that it uses for determining whether someone is a full-time employee and whether their coverage is affordable. Considering which classes of employees are offered coverage is also important to ensure that the employer is not discriminating against its lower paid employees in terms of coverage and potentially facing a discrimination issue. Essentially, legal counsel needs to determine if the client's plan is compliant with the existing health care laws. Specifically, whether the plan is ACA-compliant, if it is covering the right people, and if these people can afford it. We generally take a step-by-step approach to ACA compliance.

Another important issue in this area pertains to an analysis of ownership of the employer. While this is generally more of a tax issue, it is very important under the ACA. Basically, there are IRS rules that require that companies/entities owned by other companies/entities be considered one group for purposes of the ACA. That is, all of the employees in a group must be combined to determine whether or not the companies/entities in the group are subject to the "Play or Pay" employer mandate. For example, if ABC corporation has a subsidiary, DEF corporation, and 80 percent of DEF is owned by ABC corporation, DEF's employees will count toward ABC's total number of employees—and health insurance coverage will have to be provided to them to comply with the ACA. However, each corporation would be required to report its employees separately under Code Sections 6055 or 6056. Even if the ownership arrangement is not a straight parent-subsidiary relationship, as described above, common ownership, including at the individual-owner level, must be considered. This is a frequent occurrence with franchise arrangements where you have interlocking ownership arrangements. For example, a group of restaurants may be owned by various entities and those entities may have enough common ownership to be considered one group for purposes of the ACA. Therefore, it is important to review ownership to determine whether there is common ownership under IRS rules that would require all of the entities to be subject to the "Play or Pay" mandate.

The individuals who oversee compliance in this area will vary, depending on the type of group health plan that you are dealing with—and normally, health plan oversight represents a large expenditure. In some cases, oversight is conducted by a Senior Vice President of Human Resources who is in charge of benefits, or a company's tax or risk management group, depending on the corporate structure. Normally, the Board is aware of at least the overarching issues (e.g., it may be concerned about "Play or Pay" issues). Typically, a company will hire consultants and lawyers that are needed for conducting general oversight of ACA compliance. Legal counsel needs to assess the level of expertise of the employer to ensure that it provides the appropriate type of analysis required for that employer.

Conclusion

Health care reform is a continuing process, constantly being revised and remolded, based on new regulations, guidance, and interpretations of current laws. Decisions made in this area may be impacted by the prevailing winds of the political processes. Assisting employers with ACA compliance and the related laws requires diligent effort to stay on top of these various forces and to keep abreast of all new developments. It is important to forge a strong relationship with the employer to ensure that, as legal counsel, you have the complete picture of its health care arrangements to assist such employer in both determining whether to "Play or Pay," and if it decides to "Play," how to "Play" in a way that is legally compliant and meets its corporate goals.

Upcoming ACA Compliance Issues

Future ACA compliance issues will largely depend on what happens in the political environment. For instance, if there is a major change in control in the House, Senate, or the Presidency, that change could impact the ACA. A major issue on the horizon, is the so-called "Cadillac tax" that comes into effect in 2018. The Cadillac tax was designed to raise revenue for the ACA and to reduce employer incentive to overspend on health plans and employee incentive to overuse services encouraged by these high-cost plans. However, beyond its role as a funding mechanism, the Cadillac tax could have significant unintended consequences and be problematic for employers and multiemployer group health plans. If a Cadillac tax is assessed with respect to a plan based on an actuarial value calculation, a penalty will be required for having a plan that is "too rich in benefits." The threshold amount for 2018 is an annual actuarial value of $10,200 for single-only coverage and $27,500 for dependent coverage (to be adjusted in future years based on the Consumer Price Index). If the actuarial value is above that amount, a 40 percent excise tax is due on the amount that exceeds the threshold. For instance, if an employer's health coverage for single only employee coverage is valued at $11,200, which is $1,000 over the threshold, then the employer would pay a penalty equal to 40 percent of that amount, or $400 per employee enrolled in this coverage. As noted, multiemployer plans (specialized plans that provide benefits to certain union employees) are likely to exceed that threshold. Consequently, this is one area where employers' and unions' interests are possibly aligned because the Cadillac tax will impact the benefits provided to the employees covered under their plans.

Helping Clients Avoid Enforcement Actions/Advice for Attorneys

I believe that an attorney's role in this area is to be actively involved in making his or her clients aware of, and helping them comply with, the rules pertaining to the ACA. Attorneys also have an important role in advising clients on possible strategies under the ACA. After reading this chapter, my next point is self-explanatory—you need to practice in this area on a full-time basis. You cannot be an occasional practitioner or you may not be effective legal counsel and may harm your client's interests. Legal counsel needs to follow every new regulation, notice, or guidance that is released and read all major articles about the ACA. Also, being aware of the

Frequently Asked Questions (FAQs) that the IRS, DOL, and other implementing agencies issue on a regular basis is also critical as these FAQs provide insight into these agencies' interpretation of the ACA. In addition, you should communicate with other lawyers that practice in this area and become a member of groups, such as the American Bar Association (ABA) and the American Health Lawyers Association to stay on top of all of the ongoing changes in relation to the ACA.

Key Takeaways

- Determine if your client's group health plan is compliant with the existing health care laws and if it is ACA compliant (e.g., it is covering the right people, it is affordable to them, etc.).
- Determine how many employees may be "full-time," including exceptions to the rules, such as temporary or seasonal employees.
- Suggest that your client develop its own methodology for determining its measurement periods for every class of its employees and document its choices in   its plan records.
- Tell clients to call you immediately if they are notified of an ACA investigation or audit. Help your clients gather and review their records prior to any investigation or audit and present them in an organized manner to the investigating agency (e.g., the IRS, DOL, etc.). Attend IRS and DOL conferences to find out as much as possible about any new or potential developments in this area.
- Present webinars, issue client alerts, and conduct in-person meetings for your clients.
- Make clients aware of, and help them comply with, the rules pertaining to the ACA as they keep changing and give clients advice as to proper strategies.
- Practice in this area on a full-time basis and following every new regulation (or guidance) that is released.

Laura Miller Andrew is a partner in the executive compensation and employee benefits group at Smith Gambrell & Russell LLP, with over fifteen years of experience. Ms. Andrew advises clients in all major aspects of employee benefits including qualified and nonqualified plans, IRS and DOL compliance matters, merger and acquisition issues, executive compensation, and employment agreements. She also concentrates her practice in health care related matters, including health care reform legislation, compliance with HIPAA, and state and federal regulations impacting health care organizations, including medical device and life sciences organizations. Ms. Andrew has written and lectured extensively on many aspects of employee benefits and health care law.

APPENDICES

APPENDIX A

UNITED STATES DEPARTMENT OF JUSTICE AND HHS RECOVERIES

FOR IMMEDIATE RELEASE
February 26, 2014
Contact: HHS Press Office
(202) 690-6343

Departments of Justice and Health and Human Services announce record-breaking recoveries resulting from joint efforts to combat health care fraud Government teams recovered $4.3 billion in FY 2013 and $19.2 billion over the last five years

Attorney General Eric Holder and HHS Secretary Kathleen Sebelius today released the annual Health Care Fraud and Abuse Control (HCFAC) Program report showing that for every dollar spent on health care-related fraud and abuse investigations through this and other programs in the last three years, the government recovered $8.10. This is the highest three-year average return on investment in the 17-year history of the HCFAC Program.

The government's health care fraud prevention and enforcement efforts recovered a record-breaking $4.3 billion in taxpayer dollars in Fiscal Year (FY) 2013, up from $4.2 billion in FY 2012, from individuals and companies who attempted to defraud federal health programs serving seniors or who sought payments from taxpayers to which they were not entitled. Over the last five years, the administration's enforcement efforts have recovered $19.2 billion, up from $9.4 billion over the prior five-year period. Since the inception of the program in1997, the HCFAC Program has returned more than $25.9 billion to the Medicare Trust Funds and treasury.

These recoveries, released today in the annual HCFAC Program report, demonstrate President Obama's commitment to making the elimination of fraud, waste and abuse, particularly in health care, a top priority for the administration. This is the fifth consecutive year that the program has increased recoveries over the past year, climbing from $2 billion in FY 2008 to over $4 billion every year since FY 2011.

The success of this joint Department of Justice and HHS effort was made possible in part by the Health Care Fraud Prevention and Enforcement Action Team (HEAT), created in 2009 to prevent fraud, waste and abuse in Medicare and Medicaid and to crack down on individuals and entities that are abusing the system and costing American taxpayers billions of dollars.

"With these extraordinary recoveries, and the record-high rate of return on investment we've achieved on our comprehensive health care fraud enforcement efforts, we're sending a strong message to those who would take advantage of their fellow citizens, target vulnerable populations, and commit fraud on federal health care programs," said Attorney General Eric Holder. "Thanks to initiatives like HEAT, our work to combat fraud has never been more cooperative or more effective. And our unprecedented commitment to holding criminals accountable, and securing remarkable results for American taxpayers, is paying dividends."

"These impressive recoveries for the American taxpayer are just one aspect of the comprehensive anti-fraud strategy we have implemented since the passage of the Affordable Care Act," said HHS Secretary Sebelius. "We've cracked down on tens of thousands health care providers suspected of Medicare fraud. New enrollment screening techniques are proving effective in preventing high risk providers from getting into the system, and the new computer analytics system that detects and stops fraudulent billing before money ever goes out the door is accomplishing positive results – all of which are adding to savings for the Medicare Trust Fund."

The new authorities under the Affordable Care Act granted to HHS and the Centers for Medicare & Medicaid Services (CMS) were instrumental in clamping down on fraudulent activity in health care. In FY 2013, CMS announced the first use of its temporary moratoria authority granted by the Affordable Care Act. The action stopped enrollment of new home health or ambulance enrollments in three fraud hot spots around the country, allowing CMS and its law enforcement partners to remove bad actors from the program while blocking provider entry or re-entry into these already over-supplied markets.

The Justice Department and HHS have improved their coordination through HEAT and are currently operating Medicare Fraud Strike Force teams in nine areas across the country. The strike force teams use advanced data analysis techniques to identify high-billing levels in health care fraud hot spots so that interagency teams can target emerging or migrating schemes as well as chronic fraud by criminals masquerading as health care providers or suppliers. The Justice Department's enforcement of the civil False Claims Act and the Federal Food, Drug and Cosmetic Act has produced similar record-breaking results. These combined efforts coordinated under HEAT have expanded local partnerships and helped educate Medicare beneficiaries about how to protect themselves against fraud.

In Fiscal Year 2013, the strike force secured records in the number of cases filed (137), individuals charged (345), guilty pleas secured (234) and jury trial convictions (46). Beyond these remarkable results, the defendants who were charged and sentenced are facing significant time in prison – an average of 52 months in prison for those sentenced in FY 2013, and an average of 47 months in prison for those sentenced since 2007.

In FY 2013, the Justice Department opened 1,013 new criminal health care fraud investigations involving 1,910 potential defendants, and a total of 718 defendants were convicted of health care fraud-related crimes during the year. The department also opened 1,083 new civil health care fraud investigations.

The strike force coordinated a takedown in May 2013 that resulted in charges by eight strike force cities against 89 individuals, including doctors, nurses and other licensed medical professionals, for their alleged participation in Medicare fraud schemes involving approximately $223 million in false billings. As a part of the May 2013 takedown, HHS also suspended or took other administrative action against 18 providers using authority under the health care law to suspend payments until an investigation is complete.

In FY 2013, the strike force secured records in the number of cases filed (137), individuals charged (345), guilty pleas secured (234) and jury trial convictions (48). Beyond these remarkable results, the defendants who were charged and sentenced are facing significant time in prison – an average of 52 months in prison for those sentenced in FY 2013, and an average of 47 months in prison for those sentenced since 2007.

In March 2011, CMS began an ambitious project to revalidate all 1.5 million Medicare enrolled providers and suppliers under the Affordable Care Act screening requirements. As of September 2013, more than 535,000 providers were subject to the new screening requirements and over 225,000 lost the ability to bill Medicare due to the Affordable Care Act requirements and other proactive initiatives. Since the Affordable Care Act, CMS has also revoked 14,663 providers and suppliers' ability to bill the Medicare program. These providers were removed from the program because they had felony convictions, were not operational at the address CMS had on file, or were not in compliance with CMS rules.

HHS and the Justice Department are leading historic efforts with the private sector to bring innovation to the fight against health care fraud. In addition to real-time data and information exchanges with the private sector, CMS' Program Integrity Command Center worked with the HHS Office of the Inspector General and the FBI to conduct 93 missions to detect, investigate, and reduce improper payments in FY 2013.

From May 2013 through August 2013, CMS led an outreach and education campaign targeted to specific communities where Medicare fraud is more prevalent. This multimedia campaign included national television, radio, and print outreach and resulted in an increased awareness of how to detect and report Medicare fraud

****

What are the penalties for violating HIPAA?

The Health Insurance Portability and Accountability Act of 1996 (HIPAA) established rules protecting the privacy and security of personal health data. The HIPAA Security Rule set national standards specifically for the security of protected health information (PHI) that is created, stored, transmitted, or received electronically (i.e., electronic protected health information, or ePHI). To ensure the confidentiality, integrity, and availability of ePHI data, the HIPAA Security Rule requires organizations and individuals to implement a series of administrative, physical, and technical safeguards when working with ePHI data.

Failure to comply with HIPAA requirements can result in civil and criminal penalties, as well as progressive disciplinary actions through Indiana

University, up to and including termination. These civil and criminal penalties can apply to both covered entities and individuals.

Section 13410(D) of the HITECH Act, which became effective on February 18, 2009, revised section 1176(a) of the Social Security Act by establishing:

- Four categories of violations that reflect increasing levels of culpability;
- Four corresponding tiers of penalties that significantly increase the minimum penalty amount for each violation; and
- A maximum penalty amount of $1.5 million for all violations of an identical provision

Civil monetary penalties

Tier Penalty

4. Covered entity or individual did not know (and by exercising reasonable diligence would not have known) the act was a HIPAA violation. $100-$50,000 for each violation, up to a maximum of $1.5 million for identical provisions during a calendar year
5. The HIPAA violation had a reasonable cause and was not due to willful neglect. $1,000-$50,000 for each violation, up to a maximum of $1.5 million for identical provisions during a calendar year
6. The HIPAA violation was due to willful neglect but the violation was corrected within the required time period. $10,000-$50,000 for each violation, up to a maximum of $1.5 million for identical provisions during a calendar year
7. The HIPAA violation was due to willful neglect and was not corrected. $50,000 or more for each violation, up to a maximum of $1.5 million for identical provisions during a calendar year

Criminal penalties

Tier Potential Jail Sentence

Unknowingly or with reasonable cause: Up to one year
Under false pretenses: Up to five years
For personal gain or malicious reasons: Up to ten years

The UITS Advanced Biomedical IT Core (ABITC) provides consulting and online help for Indiana University researchers who need help securely processing, storing, and sharing ePHI research data. If you need help or have questions about managing HIPAA-regulated data at IU, contact the ABITC. For additional details about HIPAA compliance at IU, see HIPAA & ABITC and the Office of Vice President and General Counsel (OVPGC) HIPAA Privacy & Security page.

Courtesy of Terry Schneier, Lewis Brisbois Bisgaard & Smith LLP

APPENDIX B

AFFORDABLE CARE ACT INFORMATION REPORTING REQUIREMENTS

Reporting Requirement	Reporting Method	Information Reported to IRS	Information Reported to Individual	What Form to Use
IRC § 6055	Only one method (no alternatives)[1]	• Name, address, TIN for "responsible individual." • Name, address, TIN for each individual covered.[2] • Months for which each individual was covered during the calendar year. • Name, address, EIN of sponsor.	• All information reported to the IRS. • Policy number (if applicable.) • Name, address, and contact information for reporting entity.	For IRS: • 1094-C • 1095-C For Employees: • No form given yet (may be satisfied by a copy of the 1095-C given to the IRS.)

---

[1] Please note that certain large employers who provide self-insured health care coverage may be able to satisfy these reporting requirements by submitting a single form that combines the requirements of both IRC § 6055 and IRC § 6056.

[2] This also includes information coverage for retirees that are not yet 65 who remain covered on their existing health plans. Please note that employers will not have to report on the coverage for the retirees who are age 65 and older and Medicare primary.

Reporting Requirement	Reporting Method	Information Reported to IRS	Information Reported to Individual	What Form to Use	
IRC § 6056	General Method	<ul><li>Name, address, employer identification number (EIN) of the employer.</li><li>Name and telephone number of the employer's contact person.</li><li>Calendar year for which the information is reported.</li><li>Certification as to whether the employer offered its full-time employees and their dependents the opportunity to enroll in minimum essential coverage by calendar month.</li><li>Months during the calendar year that minimum essential coverage under the plan was available.</li><li>Each full-time employee's share of lowest cost premium for self-only coverage.</li><li>Number of full-time employees for each month during the calendar year.</li><li>Name, address and taxpayer identification number (TIN) of each full-time employee and the months of coverage.</li></ul>	<ul><li>All the information reported to the IRS.</li><li>Name, address, and contact information of the employer.</li></ul>	For IRS:<ul><li>1094-C</li><li>1095-C</li></ul>	For Employees:<ul><li>1095-C</li></ul>

Reporting Requirement	Reporting Method	Information Reported to IRS	Information Reported to Individual	What Form to Use
		Per Indicator Codes • Total number of employees (part time or full time). • Whether a permissible waiting period affects the months of coverage. • Information as to whether the coverage offered to full-time employees and their dependents under his or her employer's sponsored plan provides minimum value and whether the employees had the opportunity to enroll his or her spouse in the coverage. • If a third party is reporting for an employer's sponsored plan, the name, address, and identification number of the third party (in addition to the name, address, and EIN of the employer). • Information on controlled group.		

Reporting Requirement IRC § 6056	Reporting Method	Information Reported to IRS	Information Reported to Individual	What Form to Use
	Qualifying Offer	• Employee's name, social security number, and address. • Indicator code specifying that a qualified offer was made for a full 12 months to 96% of full-time employees.	General statement that the employee has received an offer of minimum essential health coverage that is affordable for the full 12 months.	For IRS: • 1094-C • 1095-C For Employees: No form given yet (may be satisfied by a copy of the 1095-C given to the IRS.)
	Special Qualifying Offer for 2015[3]	• Employee's name, social security number, and address. • Indicator code specifying that a qualified offer was made for a full 12 months to 95% of full-time employees.	General statement that the employee has received an offer of minimum essential health coverage.	For IRS: • 1094-C • 1095-C For Employees: No form given yet (may be satisfied by a copy of the 1095-C given to the IRS.)

[3] Please note that in 2015 only, if an employer provides a qualifying offer to 70% or more of its full-time employees, it will not be penalized in 2015 under section 4980H(a) (the $3,000 payment penalty), but the employer will not be able to use the simplified qualifying offer method, instead the general method will be required.

Reporting Requirement	Reporting Method	Information Reported to IRS	Information Reported to Individual	What Form to Use
IRC § 6056	98% Offer Method	• Employee's name, social security number, and address. • Indicator code specifying that a qualifying offer was made to 98% of full-time employees.	• General statement that the employee has received an offer of minimum essential health coverage that is affordable, or • General statement that the employee has received a qualified offer of coverage for less than full 12 months. • The contact name and number of the employer to obtain more information regarding the offer of coverage.	For IRS: • 1094-C • 1095-C For Employees: No form given yet (may be satisfied by a copy of the 1095-C given to the IRS.)

ASPATORE